116481

# Images of American Architecture

# Images of American Architecture

### Robert Miles Parker

Lancaster-Miller Publishers

LANCASTER - MILLER PUBLISHERS
3165 Adeline Street
Berkeley, California 94703
(415)845-3782
Cable: LANMILL


Jacket image:
Pembrook Avenue  Norfolk, Virginia
Title Page image:
F. Scott Fitzgerald's Row House
St. Paul, Minnesota


Parker, Robert Miles.
    Images of American architecture.

    1. Architecture—United States.  I. Title.
NA705 .P37      720' .973      81-8473
ISBN 0-89581-036-0            AACR2


Printed in Japan

## ACKNOWLEDGMENTS

I must thank Merika Gopaul, Peter McNames, Gayle Schmidt, Michael Main, Michael Sullivan and Stephen McCarroll for their special support while I went to see America. My greatest thank you is to Peggy McCarroll.

# Contents

*To Martha and Eddie Alf.*
*They encouraged me to make art.*

# Preface

IMAGES OF AMERICAN ARCHITECTURE is the result of a three-year pilgrimage which began as a personal fantasy. Growing up in a Navy family, I saw a lot of America. And as a Southerner, I was taught to love and cherish the South...and my country. I also, however, lived through the Sixties, when it was popular to say that America was in a decline, dying. I wondered, and worried. The worries stayed with me into the Seventies—I was an Art Therapist at a Mental Health Center in San Diego. Much of the teaching philosophy had to do with getting in touch with your fantasies. One day I heard the message. I realized that my fantasy was to travel all over the United States and see exactly what was going on.

This book, of drawings and words, is the record of what I experienced. People all over America gave me wonderful stories, and unlimited help and hospitality. In return, I hope I gave them a different view of "that shabby old building in the corner." Always a preservationist, and addicted to Victoriana, I found untold numbers of forgotten architectural gems scattered throughout the land. I prodded and proselytized everywhere I went about the importance of preserving the best, or even the worst, if unique, of our architectural past. I had my successes, and my failures. Several cities now have active preservation groups that didn't exist before, and some significant structures are still standing that might have been lost forever without the tireless efforts of those people who learned to care. About one third of the buildings that I used as subjects (383 drawings all together) are gone now, replaced by parking lots, condos, and square concrete highrises. Apathy, and the quest for profit are the destroyers of the past, and their victims are pieces of history. We, and all generations to come, are the losers in the end.

But I haven't given up. There is an enormous resurgence of interest in this country directed toward the beauties, oddities, and wonders of our past. Historic Preservation is on the upswing, and regeneration of decaying urban centers in many cities is instilling a love for the old architectural styles. Popular pressure on politicians and developers is a powerful tool. If this book, the product of more than five years work, can awaken more public interest in America's visual feast, it will have done its job, and will be my gift back to the country I love.

*Robert Miles Parker*

# The South

Johnson's Press Shop,
New Orleans, Louisiana

## Public Market
## Charleston, South Carolina

WHAT AN ELEGANT statement for a public market. Almost a centipede, reaching out with those fancy wrought-iron feelers and dragging its tail of arches behind. And what a story it could tell, of people who have stopped to buy vegetables, fresh from early morning picking; of slaves recently purchased only a block or two away, being led past the stately place. Now it is a museum for the venerable Daughters of the Confederacy.

The market lives on. Under the main structure are arty shops for tourists, but the colonnaded rear of the place still wiggles to the call of dark peddlers, selling everything from peanuts to woven baskets.

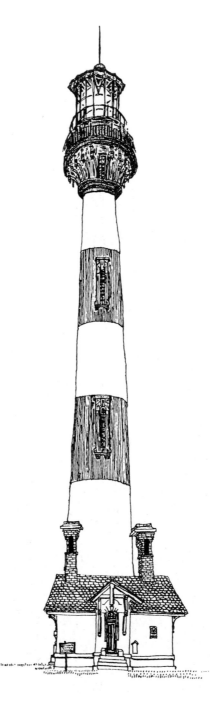

## Royal Street
## New Orleans, Louisiana

NEW ORLEANS IS billed as one of the world's unique cities. It is. You have to drive for 15 minutes to get to anyplace that feels like the rest of America. It is charming and European, and very dirty.

The Quarter is old and molding, a left-over of cultures, still living. Shoe-shine black boys walk down streets singing: "Shine, shine, now's the time." Hare Krishnas jangle their painted way along. Folk singers and old Negroes sing on corners. Sometimes the tourists sing as they amble along. The Quarter does something to you.

Horses clop by, their drivers pointing out ornamental grillwork to passenger-tourists. They tell that buildings are mostly of soft, locally made brick, laid between cypress timbers for reinforcement. The buildings are then plastered over to keep out the damp.

Mansions are two to four storeys, shops on ground floors and living quarters above. Huge cypress doors open into tunnel-corridors that lead to the courtyards. Slaves' quarters were to the sides and rear, along with stables and carriage houses.

New Orleans just exists—its uniqueness doesn't seem too special.

## Bodie Island Lighthouse
## Outer Banks, North Carolina

EVERYONE IN NORTH Carolina visits the Outer Banks. The fishing is great, the land simple and rugged. The best way to get here is to take a ferry out of the past—a two hour ride that isn't long enough. The ferries have names like the "V.S. N.C. Pamilco" and the "A. Drinkwater."

Most of the Outer Banks area is part of the Cape Hatteras National Seashore. North Carolina loves this land—it is protected from the onslaught of motels and eating stands. The lighthouse on the Outer Banks is near Roanoke Island—where in 1587, English America almost started. It was on Roanoke Island that Sir Walter Raleigh planted the settlers who began the famous Lost Colony. Built in 1872, this is the third Bodie Island lighthouse. The lens was made in Paris. The tower is 156 feet tall. There are 214 steps up spiral stairs which the keeper had to climb twice daily. Whale oil was used to create the light.

13

## New Hanover County Courthouse
## Wilmington, North Carolina

NORTH CAROLINA, I'VE always heard, is a valley of humility between two mountains of conceit. If Virginia feels like South Carolina, then it is true. North Carolina is a pleasant, gentle, and unassuming place. It is a friendly looking Sunday town with beautiful residential areas.

North Carolina has interesting things to look at everywhere: old buildings, rivers and trees, and green vistas. The State was incorporated in 1739 and given a representative in the Colonial General Assembly. The town was named for the Earl of Wilmington who sponsored the colony founded by Governor Johnson. The Governor favored the site of Wilmington and caused the Courts and Council to meet here. The city is still, and always has been, an important port between the two branches of the Cape Fear River. It was very important during the 18th and 19th Centuries, and at one time was the world's largest port for naval stores; pitch, tar resin, and turpentine.

## The First Presbyterian Church
## Port Gibson, Mississippi

PORT GIBSON IS the town that General Grant said "is too beautiful to burn." And it is another one of those charming Southern towns. There is the town hall, rows of ancient and crumbling buildings, lots of blacks sitting around, and the Presbyterian Church. Today there was a wedding. The Reverend Zebulon Butler would have been proud: booming bells (five minutes before the hour), and ladies dressed in almost the same outfits the Reverend would recognize—fluffy, sheer long dresses —chatting for a minute with their men-folk, and strolling on in. Reverend Butler was the first resident pastor. He led his flock from 1827 to 1860.

This is the second oldest Protestant Church in the old Southwest. The church first opened its door in 1807, being called the Bayou Pierre Church. It moved to Port Gibson in 1827. The present building was constructed in 1859.

Maybe General Grant saw that ominous golden hand pointing to the Divine Judge; maybe that's why he didn't burn the church and the town.

## Freemason Street
## Norfolk, Virginia

FREEMASON STREET IS one of the oldest streets in Norfolk. It was a fashionable area in the 1700's. Now it is in the process of being "revamped and redecorated." It has been through what they call Norfolk's "Bawdy Period." And it seems to be squeaking through the "Age of Redevelopment." There is only one other street in the world named "Freemason." It's in North Carolina.

Many of the most important names in American History have looked at the buildings and walked the cobblestones. The Marquis de Lafayette and his son, George Washington Lafayette; Presidents Monroe, Taft and Roosevelt, and Daniel Webster are a few of the people who have been entertained here. It's a fine old street, and, it's not even listed in the tourists' guide brochure.

16

## The Stone House
## Fayetteville, Arkansas

THERE'S A SIGN that tells about this house. It was built in 1845 by Judge David Walker. Steven K. Stone and his family moved into it in 1850. They lived there, the sign notes, before and after the Civil War. The sign further notes that a shot from Fagan's Confederate battery, in October of 1854, pierced the west wall of the house. Amanda Brodie Stone and her husband "were public spirited and gave to City Hospital, Methodist Church, and the Fayetteville Female Seminary. The Stone's daughter, Mary, was the last graduate of the Seminary in 1860."

How Southern to enshrine a house whose wall was pierced by a Civil War bullet; how charming. And how charming, too, to enshrine a family which supported such worthy causes as the Fayetteville Female Seminary. And I think it only right; I'm glad to know the house these people lived in. And I, too, would remember, and feel it worthy of note, if a war happened in my front yard.

17

## D'Evereaux
### Natchez, Mississippi

MAYBE I'M A creature of my times. I had never felt the splendor of an ante-bellum house until I drove up to the D'Evereaux steps. I wanted to stroll up those shiny steps, lean against one of the huge Doric columns, and look out at the tulips nodding under the Spanish moss. I wanted to rest a while on the porch, to think about how nicely the world is going, and just feel good. D'Evereaux was built when people felt that way. The people of Natchez, especially. Out of the 20 millionaires in America, over half "called Natchez their home." 1840 was a good time. So were the years to come after. Until the War.

People lived in a genteel manner. They prided themselves on their style. It is the same even now in Natchez. Sure, everyone is proud of their old houses. They have giant home and garden tours sponsored by the Pilgrimage Garden Club. But, most importantly, they live the old style. They are kind and gracious. The Garden Club ladies gave me lunch. One can feel the calm, the richness, just like D'Evereaux.

## Houses on Road 62B
### Eureka Springs, Arkansas

EUREKA SPRINGS HAS to be the most unique Victorian town I've seen in a long time. It is all built on hills and tumbles down into the hollers. Such a pleasant place. The town didn't come along until 1879—it was named on July 4th. The little village is scattered over 20 hills and 19 canyons. There are 238 streets, only six carry their names across intersections. Victorians wandered these crooked streets in search of the proper spring; the area is loaded with mineral springs. They came to the Crescent Hotel—still there and as ugly a Victorian pile as anyone could desire—I liked it. And they visited the Basin Park Hotel, which has eight storeys, and every floor is a ground floor. The town is billed as a Swiss Village. Where in Switzerland can one eat a good piece of huckleberry pie?

## The Fox Theatre
## Atlanta, Georgia

THE FOX THEATRE, strange and unique, is about to be destroyed. It was built in 1929, almost completed by the Shriners as a temple, then the crash came. A theatre chain bought the structure, completing it and making it a movie house. It is a real Moorish Palace; they say the pipe organ was one of the largest in the world. There are catacombs underneath. The walls were made of horse hair and all kinds of other things. The ticket booth is solid bronze. The most wonderful thing, I heard, was the ceiling —stars moved and twinkled, clouds floated by. All accomplished by special lighting techniques.

Bell Telephone bought the building for four million dollars, and it will cost another million to tear it down. Then Bell wants to build a modern structure. Atlantans are fighting to save their palace. Each day one hears that it is saved and each day one hears that it is doomed.

## The Bennett Place
## Durham, North Carolina

THIS WAS THE farm home of James Bennett. Here, on April 26, 1865, the Confederate General Johnson surrendered his army to General Sherman of the Union. The surrender followed that of General Lee at Appomattox by seventeen days. Thus the Civil War ended in the Carolinas, Georgia, and Florida. The original Bennett house burned in 1921, only the chimney was left standing. The present building is a reconstruction. "It was here that the principle of an inviolate, indissoluble Union was established. Here, also, was the last stand of the Confederacy and its belief in 'indestructible States.'" And here my family lived, here I found myself part of the great history of America.

## Corner of Church Street
## and Cedar Street
## Mobile, Alabama

THROUGH RAIN-SMEARED windows, I could see these tired and shaggy homes. Each one seemed to be a boarding house. But each had a sign: Pollock Wolley, 1904. The buildings are part of the East Church Street Historic District, an area designated to remain as it is—except to be refurbished with fresh paint and for trimmed bushes.

For some time before the Civil War, Mobile was a great city. Cotton was king. People lived lavishly. The time was called, "The Grand Ante-Bellum Era." Life was easy . . . then came the War. Alabama was the first state to secede from the Union. Reconstruction was hard and ugly—but it happened. The port was improved many times, making the city a major seaport. Industry came. Mobile grew again. These little houses are the product of that growth. They are a part of a new history and a new tradition in Alabama.

## Union Station
## Montgomery, Alabama

AND HERE'S THE South after the War. In a town full of wonderful Ante-Bellum and Victorian structures, stands this proud Union Station. It was built in the late 1800's, and could be called "Romanesque Revival." It looks like a wonderful, proud toy. Towers reaching up into the Southern sky, smoke-stacks breaking through the clouds. Pointed roofs, everywhere little windows—watching in all directions. The Union Station is on its way to being restored. Montgomery doesn't seem to be interested only in the Ante-Bellum. The city has recognized good buildings, whatever they are. And Montgomery is full of great architecture. Next to the Station is a row of excellent commercial Victorians—all are to be restored. Even the new buildings in Montgomery are okay.

22

UNION STATION

## Log Cabin
## Pickle Fork Holler, Kentucky

THERE WAS A blue sky backdropping this old log cabin. And it got bluer still as it touched the hills; those hills, brushed with coming smoky night. A hazy moon sits over my shoulder and looks on.

It's hard to find log cabins now. You have to go way up into places that still feel untouched by man: places that are as lovely as any I've seen. Still they exist. You find them in nooks and crannys in western Virginia. And they hide, in places like Pickle Fork Holler. These structures are true pioneer architecture. They blend with the woods, rising out only slightly.

There may be an outhouse sitting nearby, but that doesn't mean the country is primitive. This cabin is occupied by a middle-aged couple. You might find them sitting on the porch glider saying "howdy" and watching for occasional passers-by. Red ticks and black spiders scurry along the ground, perhaps the only hurrying critters in those hills. You know, never to judge a book by its cover. That gentleman with his country drawl and his brittle wife were once uptown New Yorkers. The same gentleman is a graduate of the Julliard School of Music.

## Company Store No. 5
## Upper Van Lear, Kentucky

IT WAS A hot Saturday afternoon, so hot that about all you could do was perch on that old railing and drink Pepsi-Cola, maybe eat a popsicle. That's what Loretta used to do. It's Herman Webb's store now. But once the building was Company Store No. 5. The Consolidation Coal Company was the owner. Inside is the usual conglomeration of flour sacks, canned goods, the ice cream bin, cracker barrels, and other stuff. Hanging on the wall, somewhere behind the old wooden counter, is a calendar with Loretta Lynn's picture on it. Herman is Loretta's brother, and they were born in Upper Van Lear Holler just a stone's throw from the store, in a log cabin, too. Herman worked in the coal mining factories. But they've closed. Now he's returned to run this store.

And while I was there Loretta Lynn came to visit. She's history too. She's from those hills and hollers, and she's "made it." The people back home love her and respect her. She sings about the country, the problems and the life. Loretta Lynn, and Co. Store No. 5 are America. They are our tradition and our culture. And they are good.

## The Hensley Trailer
## Sitka, Kentucky

I LOVE THE hills and hollers of Eastern Kentucky. The people, too. Maybe you wouldn't think of a trailer as typical for the area, but it is. Trailers (they call them mobile homes) have become major American residential architecture. People can't really afford, any more, the down payments and the interest charges on homes planted into the ground. Trailers are ugly, I know.

When you walk inside the Hensley House, you leave behind look-alike America. The hill people still exist. Their accents and their false teeth, and their breakfasts of eggs and sausage and sorghum mixed with margarine are *de Rigeur.* What you do is, take a giant plate (which probably doesn't match any other plate), wash it with water that you carried in from Paintsville (ten miles away), and you serve all that food on it. Then after you eat, you sit and talk and smoke a lot of cigarettes. Often discussion centers around "spooks and boogers." Kentucky country people really believe in spirits. Ghosts abound, and at night, make visitations not only to old shacks up the road, but even modern homes like this one. Herman talks about the night not too long ago when a "booger" was seen at the front window. It was easy to see him because the curtains had fallen down a couple of months before. Spooks are something to be dealt with just as seriously as the sewer-stream in front of the Hensley trailer.

No matter. It's all gone now. The trailer burned down last August.

## The Fontainebleau
## Miami Beach, Florida

MIAMI BEACH AND the Fontainebleau, so what's not to like? When the hotel was built it was considered one of the great new hotels of the world, it still is.

One can swim in a huge, saltwater pool and pretend to be James Bond, knowing that the Goldfinger lady is up on one of those balconies. One can go ice skating, swim in the 78° Atlantic (private beach, of course), and eat in the Gigi Room, where you may possibly get the best service in Miami. The Gigi is done all in reds and pinks—great swashes of draped lipstick colours. There are other rooms with other high class names: the Chez Bon Bon, the Fleur de Lis, and the Poodle Room. Everyone adores, simply adores the Poodle Room. All around the walls are beautiful, "hand painted" paintings of poodles (that's right, poodles) in various French poses. And the Lobby, now there's a place—golden columns, mother-of-pearl columns, and an area to play backgammon.

The Fontainebleau is the essence of the '50's. It is pure Marilyn Monroe, pure kitsch. The circular structure was designed in 1954 by Morris Lapidus—called the King of Kitsch. His critics say he's bad. He chuckles all the way to the bank.

## Main Street Row House
## Ronceverte, West Virginia

I KNOW EXACTLY why people are always writing songs about West Virginia. Its mountains and its river are unique, they feel like home. Maybe the feeling comes from the State's location: it isn't exactly Northern, nor is it Southern; and there isn't too much of it.

Like Ronceverte, towns are mostly small. They tend to appear at the bend of a road, or at the edge of a great mountain. Each town seems independent, a legacy from the original settlers. The State was originally part of Virginia. Everyone knows that. But not many people know that the Westerners were taxed unfairly (cattle were taxed higher than slaves and slaves were counted for legislative representation in far-away Richmond). The War was a great time for those 40 western counties (who were more oriented to river trade, not Tidewater) to break away. They left Virginia and the Confederacy in 1863. Yet the people and their architecture retain much of the soft gentility of the South. They take their time and they talk real slow.

One old lady in this row house has been around for 68 years, and the house was there before her time. It was right nice 'til the owner died and his ornery son didn't keep it up. It's condemned now—the place is slowly emptying of people. In West Virginia, in a town of Huckleberry boys with fishing poles over their backs, time drifts along.

27

## Jackson County Courthouse
## Ripley, West Virginia

HERE, IN A real typical small American town is a real typical American courthouse. It embodies all the principles we have been taught. There is a little of the Renaissance in the first floor, a comment on the value of learning. Above the first level it's all Greek. Democracy with daisies. And on the top, a nice wooden lantern with a silver painted dome.

In June, in Ripley, it's "hotter than the devil out, gonna burn the tomatoes all to pieces." But that's okay, everyone is looking forward to July Fourth, "they really have a time, one of the biggest fireworks shows you'd ever want to see—right on the courthouse green."

## The Savoy Plaza
## South Miami Beach, Florida

JUST AS THE Fontainebleau is the essence of Miami in the '50's and the '60's, so the Savoy Plaza must have been in the '20's and '30's. The Savoy sits amid the decay of South Miami Beach. South Beach is nothing like the beaches to the north. No magic names like The Doral, The Fountainebleau, or the Sans Souci.

South Beach is built on a human scale. The people of the area, the old Jewish people speaking strange languages and wearing tinted green hair, talk to you and to each other. The place is tired and old, but it is alive and fun. I think the city fathers are talking about tearing all of South Beach apart—perhaps making a new North Beach down there. How sad. I don't know where all the yentas will go. And so, the old women who push walkers in front of them and talk about "my son the doctor," may be a passing thing. The once-grand hotels with pink flamingo sculptures might soon be as lost as other parts of our culture.

29

## Flagler College
## St. Augustine, Florida

THE CITY WAS founded in 1565. It has (unlike most other cities in America) undergone constant refinement. The people live aesthetically. There are no shopping centers. The Town Hall is an old hotel. Everybody just restores everything—or they build old things anew.

Of the 60 million Flagler invested in Florida, he considered this to be his grandest statement. The college was built as a hotel. The architects were John Carere and Thomas Hastings of New York. They were only in their 20's when they designed the structure. Even at the beginning (it was built in the '80's) there were electric lights and steam heat. The interior is outlandishly spectacular—huge carved ladies in the entry and paintings on the walls and ceilings. The Paintings were done by George Maynard. Tiffany created windows and chandeliers. The hotel cost $2.5 million to build and was constructed on a marsh filled with tons of sand. It was built of coquina shell composite mixed with cement—and gets harder with age. The Flagler was among the grand hotels of the world. It cost one hundred dollars a night and saw such guests as Presidents Cleveland, Harding and Roosevelt; Will Rogers, the Astors and the Rockefellers. In the late '60's the hotel was converted to Flagler College, a liberal arts institution with only 500 students.

30

## The Don CeSar Hotel
## St. Petersburg, Florida

ST. PETERSBURG BEACH was the Florida I was looking for. Millions of Miami-type high rises, beautiful beaches, and palm trees everywhere. One building: the Don CeSar, stood out. The hotel was completed in 1927. I'm sorry about the silly Spanish front they had to add, but it's a lot better than another ordinary plastic hotel.

The hotel was opened in 1928. The colour was "rouge." Ladies were resplendent in sequins and plumes. In the '40's the building became an Air Force convalescent center. Then, when the Air Force left, the old hotel almost fell apart. The Don CeSar was saved by a group of militant, determined preservationists.

## House with Trees,
## Eaton Street
## Key West, Florida

SOMETIMES, IN KEY West, the buildings stand, hot and alone, wrapped in the tropical air. And the other times, that air is made manifest in trees and bushes, palms and flowers.

## Ca'd'Zan
## Sarasota, Florida

JOHN AND MABLE Ringling's house is a carnival, a circus; how appropriate. If you sit long enough and just watch the building, you can hear the laughter of all the people who played there. People whose portraits are painted onto the ceiling of the third floor game room, painted in outrageous costumes of the Twenties— dressed as roosters, or peacocks, or maybe as clowns and wild animal trainers. The center portraits are John and Mable Ringling, of course.

The house was built in the '20's. The Ringlings liked Venice, and this is the answer to their affection. Mable had a gondola that would bring the laughing guests up to the marble wharf, and when they were helped ashore, here's what they saw: each window- pane is a different shade of coloured glass; each column is carved with little lambs' heads on the top. A row of lions growl out from the roof. Ladies hold up lamps; statues grin under lamps that are supported by cow's heads and horses' hooves.

The interior is an amazing collection of beautiful furniture from all over the world. It is rich, and at the same time, amusing. I didn't feel overwhelmed—just delighted. (Well, maybe a little overwhelmed.) The parlour is three storeys high, with a balcony that looks down from the second storey. And you don't have to sit outside too long to know that all the excitement, all the laughter, is still there.

As evening pulls out its blues and pinks, it sets the stage for a return: the building beckons, pelicans wink, or is it the statues?

## Duval Street
## Key West, Florida

THE DRIVE TO KEY WEST is exciting. The Atlantic on one side, the Gulf on the other—and you on a bridge. Beautiful water, turquoise and blue, hinting about the town at the end of the road. Suggesting a place where pirates once lived; where Hemingway did some of his writing. President Truman often vacationed in Key West, and Truman Capote calls the Island his home.

Once you get beyond those horrible shopping centers that seem to embrace every town, you find yourself in a special place. It is the southernmost city in America, and it feels it—hot and sticky. Buildings are either choked with vines and trees, or they stand starkly on the old streets.

These houses are bright white and filled with Cubans. (Not the new Cubans; these people have been part of the island since the cigar making days.) The architecture, mostly from the Victorian period, reflects a blend of Nassau, New Orleans, and Ante-Bellum. It all mixes in a strange, almost sinister, way.

Buildings that aren't hidden by palms and bushes hide behind jalousied windows, or simply wrap themselves in the sub-tropic heat.

And it's a good thing that the buildings hide. The city is still a pirate town. The little island-city has the second highest crime rate in all of Florida. It is a sophisticated town, too. Where else can one be served a drink by the pool, which is in a court-yard surrounded by thirteen conch houses, and the host looks just like Irene Dunn?

## The Windsor Hotel
## Americus, Georgia

THE WINDSOR HOTEL was started in 1878, completed in 1890, and was closed July 1974. "These people here, they can't pay no two or three hundred a month." It was built as a winter resort, long before Florida was the place to go. John Dillinger stayed here, so did President Roosevelt.

The townspeople are very proud of their hotel. Some people think "that young man from the North" (Stanford White) designed the structure. Who ever did design it really did some work. It combines every kind of architecture I've ever seen. There's a Norman tower, New Orleans French roofs here and there, commercial Victorian arches, and a few Renaissance friezes. The complete structure is a block large. It has 100 rooms, a huge ballroom, three private dining rooms, a ladies' music room (Ladies' Parlour), and a men's smoking room.

If the hotel looks friendly that is only because it reflects the town. The barber came out of his shop and gave me some bubble gum. The druggist showed me a picture of the building as it used to look. An old gentleman with a cane bought me a coke because it was a hot afternoon . . .and the building might get saved. There have recently been lots of meetings; people want to preserve their landmark. Maybe the creeping conformity I feel everywhere won't get the Windsor.

35

## The Clusky House
## Savannah, Georgia

WHAT A BEAUTIFUL building, so simple and so perfect. The balance is breathtaking. The building is called a pair house, both sides being identical in design and owned by different families. The structure was built in 1840. It is considered the finest pair of row houses of the period. The Savannah historical people rate the building as "exceptional."

36

## The Grand Ole Opry
## Nashville, Tennessee

THE GRAND OLE Opry building is a shrine to all country people. They come in droves to stand reverently and gaze at this Romanesque horror.

People listened to the Opry on crystal sets in the old days. Country singers all twanged their wares from the old Opry House. Now, of course, there's a new building. Modern, and not the least reflective of the art it houses. There are so many parking lots around the new structure that I never could find the entrance. The new place has a wooden square cut from the stage floor of the old Opry House, and it has some of the pews, too. I was told that the town has lots of new auditoriums, (making this building obsolete) and besides that "the roof leaks." But it was whispered to me that the new theatre is not as good. The oval interior of this structure boasts "the best acoustics in the U.S. except for the Mormon Tabernacle." The hollow auditorium is a natural for country music. There's nothing to absorb the sound. Everything is wooden: foors, ceilings, walls, and seats. I hate to say it, but like so many of our shrines, the structure was to be torn down. A replica one tenth the size was to be built.

Sarah Bernhardt has been there, so has Caruso.

37

# The East

**Broad Street
Newark,
New Jersey**

## Broad Street
## Newark, New Jersey

NEWARK IS AN architectural sleeper. Structures ranging from Regency to Second Empire, Mansard to Queen Anne are jumbled together all over town. They stick their heads up through noisome squalor. Only ten blocks away from this row of buildings is the oldest house in Newark.

Newark is the State's largest city and is considered one of the most distressed urban areas in the Country. New Jersey itself is the most densely populated State in the Union. There is an average of almost one thousand persons per square mile. The inner city is mostly bereft of whites. Hanging out windows and loitering on tired stoops, are black immigrants from the South, and Puerto Ricans escaping their Caribbean island. They are a mingle of shouts and yells. They don't care about nothin' but having a good time.

The State of New Jersey was first settled by the Dutch in 1630, and became British in 1664. During the Revolution, New Jersey was the scene of over 100 skirmishes and battles. In the Civil War era, there was much pro-slavery sentiment, and one can still feel it. After the Civil War, industrial expansion created the glory that was Newark. It was a wealthy place at that time, as you can see by these almost ghosts.

## The Federal Capitol Building
## Washington, D.C.

THERE IT IS, our Federal Capitol, symbol of one of the grandest Nations ever to exist. Maybe confused, certainly turbulent. I'm not so sure it's bad—that churning atmosphere. This is a country in flux. It's not hard to see that flux, and the wonder and aspirations of our founders are apparent, too.

The Capitol was officially begun when George Washington laid the cornerstone on September 18, 1793. The structure was based on a design of Dr. William Thornton, and revised by Benjamin Latrobe. The Capitol was completed in 1906.

Washington is a strange place. The people there, strolling on broad avenues and dodging crumbling slums, are quite businesslike. They don't wear jewelry; they don't smile too much; but they do dress up in suits and vests. It's a business town.

Pierre L'Enfant, who had come to the United States as a protege of Lafayette, was retained by George Washington to draw up the plans for the city. L'Enfant was assisted by Benjamin Banneker, a Negro. They envisioned a city of grand boulevards and vistas. Sometimes their vision works, sometimes it doesn't. How appropriate that a black was in on the groundwork. It's his people who really run the place, you know.

## Don Canty's House
## Cleveland Park, Washington, D.C.

CLEVELAND PARK IS an area of rambling summer resort-type houses. It was named in honor of President Grover Cleveland and was sort of an outlying suburb from bustling downtown Washington. The homes were built around the turn of the Century, reflecting the "modern style." People were interested in getting away from the formality of Victorian living. These big homes were designed for a more comfortable life-style. The feeling is very American.

Cleveland Park fell into decay in the '20's. The huge houses became apartments and places with "rooms to let." During the Kennedy era, people rediscovered the Park. Today it is a place for big trees and lots of dogs and cats. Young Moderns pursue aesthetic careers and raise healthy children.

42

## Rock of Salvation Church
## Rahway, New Jersey

IN THIS DENSELY people-packed edge of New Jersey, Rahway is the last town. The awful strip of people starts way up at Patterson and ends with little Rahway. What a strange town it is. Rahway is an ancient place and it reminded me of a rotting English village: there are little twisted streets that sprout sooty and jumbled brick buildings. There is a decay in the air, a tired and wornout feeling. Rahway appears to be all that we have learned about the East. Some of our earliest history occurs in Rahway. But that isn't as interesting as its current style.

43

**House on Rhode Island Avenue
House One Street Away
from Rhode Island Ave.
Washington, D.C.**

THESE HOUSES ARE all pretty similar: real brick rows.

## Fountain Elms
## Utica, New York

SOMETHING STRANGE HAPPENS here when you leave New England and come into Central New York. The towns have a poor look. I don't understand it. Utica and the other big cities seem to reflect that same despairing attitude; it's all so gray.

There's a street in Utica that is an oasis; Genesee Street, where Fountain Elms, an Italian Villa built in 1850, is open to visit. Designed by William L. Woollett Jr., Fountain Elms was the home of James Watson Williams. When the family members passed on to their rewards, the "Munson-Williams-Procter Institute" was created. Fountain Elms, and a modern school of art designed by Philip Johnson are part of that Institute. The Johnson building, they call "essentially classic with balanced proportions and scrupulous detail." It looks ridiculous next to stately Fountain Elms.

## Trinity Cathedral
## Newark, New Jersey

THE CATHEDRAL IS a haven of Colonial quiet surrounded by a bustling, and often filthy, modern city. It rests in a little park, murmuring of a time past.

Washington passed by in 1776, looking up, I am sure, at the tower. The first church was built in 1746. The present edifice was constructed in 1809. The tower is original.

45

## Charles Herrington's House
## Rhode Island Ave.
## Washington, D.C.

CHARLES HERRINGTON'S HOUSE was built in 1886 by William Ewans. It was part of a neighborhood that was wealthy through the '80's. From the beginning the area was racially mixed. There was a slow transition from a racial blend of residents to mostly rich blacks. Around 1900, the moneyed whites moved to the west: the bigger houses of Massachusetts Avenue. And around the same time, the places began to have public use as opposed to residential. Legations (Korea and Venezuela), and a sanatorium became neighborhood fixtures. Deterioration continued, and the wealthy left their homes to become sad old boardinghouses. As recently as 1968 the area was part of those riots that erupted all over the country. Young people like Herrington have discovered the shabby area, and have begun to move in. It's now an exciting conglomeration of tight-pants fellows painting old window shutters, Negroes sloppy with wine sitting in dank stoops, and young professionals chit-chatting and having afternoon drinks together. There's a ways to go, but it looks like these Washingtonians know the direction.

## Schnyder House
## Quogue, Long Island, New York

SURELY AN OUTLANDISH building. It makes one think of Charles Addams. In fact, Mr. Addams only lives down the road a piece, in a house that's not half so haunting. This was originally a laundry house for the front building, and is now the hospitable Schnyder House, where they serve a most bracing scotch and soda.

47

48

## View from a Waverly Place Room
## Greenwich Village
## New York City, New York

IT'S CROWDED, So crowded in New York. The people that have this view are considered lucky—they have some space to look at. And out one tiny window are 50 windows looking back.

From the front window of the same apartment, you can see the house where O. Henry lived, and the house Ruth McKenney once shared with her sister Eileen.

## Cast-Iron Building in Soho
## New York City, New York

"No Plumb is needed, no square, no level. As far as the pieces may be handled, they may be adjusted and secured by the most ignorant workman; the building cannot fail to be both perpendicular and firm." So says James Bogardus, who built the first cast-iron building in 1848. He might have added some word about how the style lends itself to a borrowing from most any culture. Cast-iron structures seem to have delightful balance and rhythm. This building is one of many in Soho district, all are a pleasure to see. The shadows alone, the way they change as the day goes by, are wonderful.

## The Pines, Fire Island
## Long Island, New York

The Pines is the posh part of Fire Island. The buildings, many of them, are designers' masterpieces. It is the great escape-place, especially for people from the Upper East Side of New York City.

49

## Stroud Mansion
## Stroudsburg, Pennsylvania

ON THE SITE where this house now stands, Benjamin Franklin (in 1756) ordered Fort Hamilton to be built. It was one of a chain of frontier forts for the providence of Pennsylvania. The three-and-a-half storey, stucco-covered stone house was built for Daniel Stroud by his father, the founder of the town. It is a simple, yet stately home, reflective of early Pennsylvania attitudes. Those attitudes are hospitable, like the Mansion. We were invited in—out of the cold—by friendly people across the street. We had a good dinner, and a song was written about us and our travels.

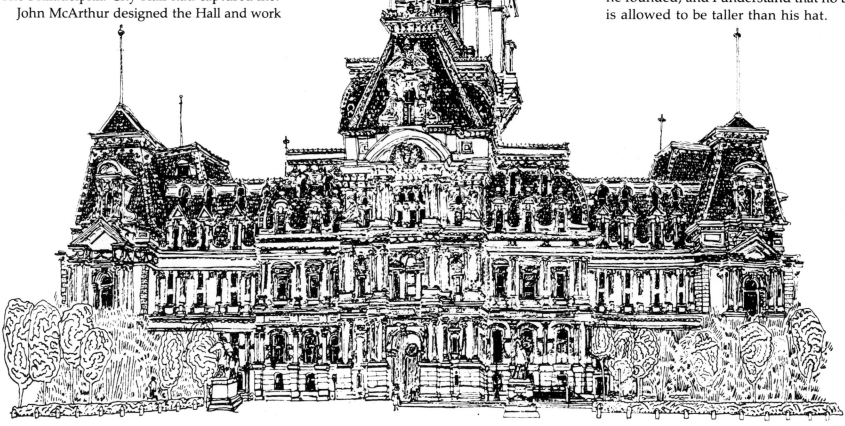

I DROVE INTO Philadelphia on a lovely Spring evening. The city began on the other side of the New Jersey bridge, in a blaze of lights. I turned onto what seemed to be the main street and began driving towards the center of town. That's always a good way to get oriented. As I drove along, Philadelphia became more and more beautiful. Near the heart, twinkling lights appeared on street trees. And in front of me loomed the most glowing building I've seen. The Philadelphia City Hall had captured me.

John McArthur designed the Hall and work began in 1871. It is considered one of the grandest American public buildings in the Second Empire Style. The style is mad: Mid-century architects figured that no school of architecture was good enough alone, so they just took a little piece from here and a hunk from there and put it all together. The grandeur of the structure is similar to Philadelphians and their attitude, a not so subtle elegance.

William Penn laid out the original plans for the city in 1682, making it the first planned city in the New World. It was a center of culture, industry and political activity. Mr. Penn stands on top of City Hall, looking over the city he founded, and I understand that no building is allowed to be taller than his hat.

51

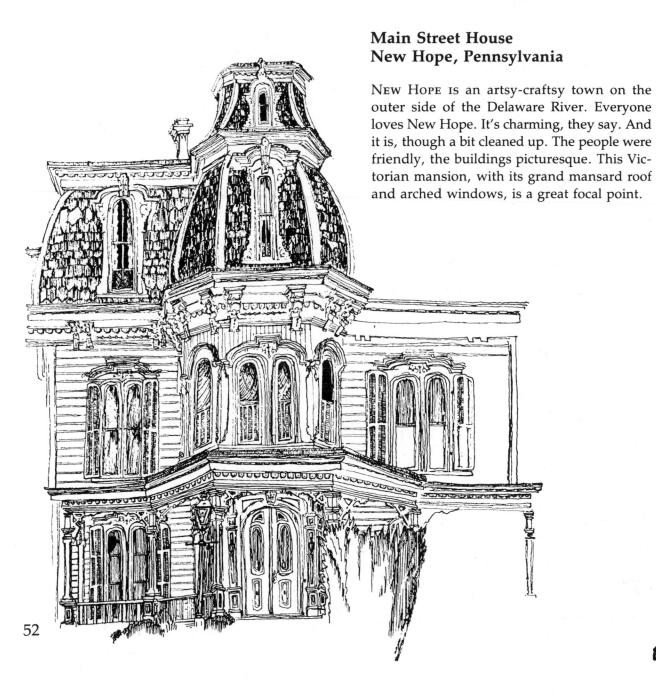

### Main Street House
### New Hope, Pennsylvania

NEW HOPE IS an artsy-craftsy town on the outer side of the Delaware River. Everyone loves New Hope. It's charming, they say. And it is, though a bit cleaned up. The people were friendly, the buildings picturesque. This Victorian mansion, with its grand mansard roof and arched windows, is a great focal point.

## The Diner
### Wilmington, Delaware

RIGHT BY WILMINGTON, one of our nation's oldest cities, is this monument to the future. Probably built before the time of junk food, places like this suggested to the weary traveler the essence of streamlined home cooking. You could be sure that somebody named Mabel had just made fresh apple pies, and that the coffee would be strong and good.

The Diner was built to reflect America's Great Technology. Stainless Steel wraps around a hull: one is tempted to think of an aeroplane or an ocean liner. Or a railroad car.

Once sleek and stylish, diners now look a little passe, but one could almost suggest that they, with the passage of time, have become not only stylishly obsolete, but strangely human.

## The Gaiety Theatre
## Baltimore, Maryland

THE GAIETY THEATRE began as a legitimate Burlesque house. It was a true pleasure palace and a passerby knew from the grandeur of the building and the carved ornamentation, that just inside those doors he could escape to a world much nicer than his dreary own.

The masks of comedy and tragedy, now dripping from pigeons, and the crumbling faces butressing windows and columns are not only ornamentation. Ugly though they may appear to the modernist, I find them comforting...human.

The poor Gaiety has a quizzical look now. Some people say it's about to be destroyed; some people want it restored. The interior of the theatre burned in 1964. That part of the building is now hollow and haunted. But even in such a state, one can feel the color, the flashing and throbbing colors of East Baltimore Street. There's still a spirit, perhaps tawdry now, but very much alive.

At street level lights and signs and bar-barkers shout for your attention: "Live Show here, see two movies in a show." "Hey buddy, come on in. Hot live show inside..."

54

## Peter Herdic Mansard
## Williamsport, Pennsylvania

WILLIAMSPORT IS NOT listed in any book I've read. I don't know why. I have never seen as large a city with so many marvelous buildings. The whole place should be declared a National Site. I think Mansard must have been born here. There are so many Mansard roofs in Williamsport.

The town moved slowly until a lumber boom in the 1870's. It was that boom that created the marvelous Victorian city which still exists. This three-storey dwelling was built about 1875, designed by Eber Culver for Peter Herdic. It is a double house—architectural detail and porch trim are different on each side of the building. It's a great house: but then there are millions of great houses in old Williamsport.

## Society Hill, 634, 636, 638 Spruce Street
## Philadelphia, Pennsylvania

SOCIETY HILL HAS certainly gone through some changes. Bobbie Schwartz can remember living in #638, sleeping in the condemned fourth floor. His parents were poor Jewish immigrants. The neighborhood itself was a melting pot of people who had deserted Europe.

Bobbie Schwartz wound up in Tuscon, and owns the biggest jewelry and pawn shop in the Southwest. From his poolside cactus garden, it's pleasant to reflect on an American success story.

# New England

"Motif #1," Rockport
**Bear Skin Neck, Massachusetts** 57

## "Motif #1," Rockport
## Bear Skin Neck, Massachusetts

BEAR SKIN NECK was settled in 1630, not too long after the Pilgrims arrived at Plymouth. It is, without any doubt, a most picturesque place. This particular view is world-famous. The area was the commercial and shipbuilding center of Rockport for 150 years. The first dock was built in 1743.

The area boasted a Stone Fort and the Sea Fencibles Barrack during the War of 1812. The far end of the point is the site of the fort. The frigate, "Nymph," captured the fort and dismantled it. Ammunition gone—all nine Sea Fencibles taken prisoner, the townsmen hurled rocks at the British, using their stockings as slings.

## The Grist Mill
## Ashland, New Hampshire

I HAVE ALWAYS thought of the West—the desert mountains, the strange land of Utah, as the most beautiful scenery in America. New Hampshire has changed my mind. I have never seen anything as overpowering as Autumn New England. The people are not as somber as I had been taught. How can they be—with these colours and buildings? They are reserved, and perhaps a bit quiet, they are like this old grist mill—rugged and well-used.

## The Ash Street School
## Manchester, New Hampshire

THEY BUILT SCHOOLS proudly in those days, monuments to education. The Ash Street School reflects the industrial sounds one always hears with the name "Manchester." The great cotton and woolen mills started in Manchester in 1838. The town was chosen as a speculative venture by the merchants of Boston—and a city grew. Now it is rather dingy and dirty—like one would expect a New England mill town to be.

In just ten years, the Amoskeag Company turned a village of 125 into a city of 10,000. The Amoskeag became the world's largest textile manufacturing plant—turning out cloth at 50 miles per hour.

But it is all over now, and most of the mills have been destroyed. The Chicopee Mill, the last operating company, closed its doors in March of 1975. The Ash Street School is one of the last reminders of Manchester's contribution to the American Industrial Revolution. 59

### The Homestead
### Sugar Hill, New Hampshire

IT WAS HERE the real meaning of harvest came to me. Getting in the crops ahead of cold winter; building defenses against the dreary time to come. The homes of New England tell that story. They reflect the hardness of winter. They lean, and they creak, yet they stand strong and resolute.

The Homestead is the oldest structure in little Sugar Hill. The first part, built in 1802, was only a primitive shelter with a fireplace. A partition for "mother and father" was the first growth of the house. In 1881, "Grandmother" took in the first guests.

That's Essie Serifini talking, and she knows more about this part of the country than anyone: "It was absolutely primitive here when Moses Aldrich came. Grandma Sara Aldrich had the pioneer spirit. She drove an ox and a cow, took eight days to get here...Had the baby, dug the first well and it's still in operation ...Everyone's down in Sugar Hill cemetery now. I just laid my husband to rest there. I'll be there too...We used to see the old folks through, in the home; today you see them out."

### Sheldon Street
### Providence, Rhode Island

SOME OF THE houses are restored, and live with the safe designation: Historic Site. A few of the buildings are really not very old. And some are considered almost slums, probably destined for demolition. The whole group sits together nicely. Because a famous name lived in a building, that building has a greater life expectancy. It seems to me we are visually doomed as long as we rely on extra-criteria to validate a piece of architecture. These places look fine together. I don't know why they are not equal in the eyes of the law.

## White Horse Tavern
## Newport, Rhode Island

IT'S A SURPRISE to find an ancient Newport. One always associates the town with rich people's mansions. There's a main street in Newport which cuts the town in two. On one side are the mansions, and on the other, one can find a rather intact community of old structures. One of those buildings is the White Horse Tavern, built in 1673.

## West Canton Street
## Boston, Massachusetts

THIS AREA, THOUGH Victorian, still has that proper Boston look. Even the slums around the corner look proper. The Puritans never died—200 years later, their legacy was still reflected in the architecture of the city.

The area where these row houses now stand was once a bay. It was filled in during the 1850's, and named the South End. The structures were built in the 1860's. The South End was quite popular for 25 years, until approximately 1895. Fashionable Back Bay was filled in the 1870's, and people began to desert the South End for the newer area...new ethnic groups moved in: the Polish, Irish, Jews, and Syrians first. Later came the Blacks and Puerto Ricans. Now, only a block away, one hears mostly Spanish, and stumbles over trash and broken buildings.

When the original owners moved they kept their old buildings—renting them to the newcomers. West Canton was lucky, most occupants remained the owners. The block is still Irish.

The building style is a direct descendent of Beacon Hill architecture, and the whole area is now an Historic Site. The buildings can't be tampered with, except to bring them back to their 1860's style. It is exciting to see the change, to see people moving back to the city and living with their past.

## Gilbert Stuart's Birthplace
## Rhode Island

OVER A BRIDGE, and west of Newport, sits a nice old house. The gambrel-roofed building surrounded by all shapes and colours of trees, feels a part of the land. Built around the 1750's, with its accompaniment of ancient stream and gnarled bridges, it bespeaks itself of timelessness.

The place is a wilderness, and the sounds are ageless. If you sit by the water all you hear are rustling leaves and perhaps a fish jumping. Gilbert Stuart was born in this little house, and it is Stuart who is to become the image-maker of George Washington.

## The Goult-Pickman House
## Salem, Massachusetts

IN MASSACHUSETTS, GOD was vengeful, and his vengeance was most terrible in Salem... you can feel it in this house. Witches float still, carefully avoiding gas stations and neon-smeared modern structures. They like houses like the Goult-Pickman House. It was built before 1660, and is one of the oldest in the town. The style is "English-Elizabethan," reflecting the colonists' homeland.

## The Buckman Tavern
## Lexington, Massachusetts

HERE'S WHERE IT all really began. This is the place where the British tried to stop the "Americans." It was at Lexington that the shot was fired that was heard around the world.

Massachusetts had been struggling to keep a self-government formed in 1774. It was a provincial government partially established to collect taxes and military supplies. King George had forbidden all town meetings called without his express permission, making the Massachusetts Provincial Congress quite illegal. But the Congress went on. Town militia groups began to do military drills. The men felt they could be formed at a minute's notice; thus the Minute Men.

In Boston, the English General Gage, Commander of that city, heard about hidden supplies in Concord. He thought revolt was in the air, and ordered 700 men to march to the town and seize the supplies. Paul Revere heard about the march and rode from Boston to Lexington to warn the colonists. Then, with two friends, he headed for Concord. An advance force of British captured Revere; one friend made his way back to Lexington, and the other ran on to warn Concord. Under Captain Parker, the Lexington militia was called to assemble. But there had been no confirmation of Revere's message, and Parker dismissed the men with the rejoiner, "reassemble at the beat of the drum." With the arrival of Thad Bownam at 4:15, Parker had definite word that the British were coming...William Diamond, the drummer-boy, went to the Common and started a noise that was to rumble ever louder. In the tavern and around the town, the men responded, gathering in the April morning.

It was Springtime, 1775. Sgt. Monroe lined the militia into two ranks, and the drum roll began. Major Pitcairy, leader of the British force, weary from his march, heard the sound as a challenge to battle and ordered his troops to load and prime their weapons. Pitcairy commanded the Rebels to lay down their arms about the same time Parker commanded them to go home (they were quite outnumbered). Then, from somewhere, a shot; and the war had begun. The British troops began firing without orders—"some ran into the Rebels, shooting and bayonetting." Eight Americans died in the first forcible armed resistance to the Crown.

## The Old State House
## Boston, Massachusetts

LIKE A PROUD ship, sailing evermore, it still stands. From the bow of this ship, from the balcony of the State House, in 1789, George Washington acknowledged the cheers of his Northern compatriots. Here, in 1781, the surrender of Cornwallis at Yorktown was proclaimed. It was from the same place that Bostonians were read the Declaration of Independence; an act that still occurs each year. These windows watched the first blood spill onto a soil that demanded freedom; the Boston Massacre.

The State House held the council chamber used by colonists' governors and the Royal Governors of England. Royal edicts were read from the balcony. In the ex-Royal Chamber, John Hancock was sworn in as the first Governor of Massachusetts. The first State House was constructed in 1657. It burned in 1711, and in 1713 the present building was constructed. In front of the building were the whipping posts, stocks, pillories, and markets. The building had outgrown its use by 1798, and government offices were moved to the New State House.

67

## Nehemiah Strong House
## Amherst, Massachusetts

How Beautiful are the fall colours framed against old wooden buildings. Maples dressed in mauves, oranges, reds; the oaks in rusts and browns. The Nehemiah Strong House rests in those colours, in gentle Amherst. The building is the oldest structure in town. It was built in 1744, and is a typical Colonial building, a gambrel-roofed frame dwelling. It was constructed by local craftsmen using hand-hewn timber and hand-wrought hardware.

Amherst is a college town now, the site of both Amherst college, and the University of Massachusetts. It's a quiet, typical New England town.

The town wasn't really founded on such gentleness. Lord Jeffrey Amherst, it is said, was a cruel man. Under the guise of friendship, Lord Jeffrey gave blankets to the local Indians. (It was a cold winter, and the good nobleman was concerned for the natives' well-being.) The blankets were not only warm, they were loaded with smallpox germs. All the Indians died.

## Meeting House
## Concord, Massachusetts

WHEN THE BRITISH were done with Lexington, they marched on towards Concord, a charming town with the past made gentle. Unlike Lexington, which has succumbed to the modern age, and is littered with neon and feels like the New World cashing in on the Old, Concord holds its past with dignity. One feels the New England character, the place looks the way it should.

It was known that military supplies were hidden in Concord—four Companies were ordered to go and destroy those supplies. The soldiers didn't find much, but started a fire anyway. The fire spread to the Town Meeting House. The British put out the fire, causing thick smoke to mar the April morning. On a hill overlooking the old North Bridge, about 400 colonists watched. They watched the troops when they came to town; they watched as the British marched over the bridge; and they could see the guard which was left to protect the bridge. The colonists saw the billowing smoke, and Joseph Hismer shouted, "Will you let them burn the town down?" Captain Isaac Davis answered, "No, I haven't a man who is afraid to go!" The 100 man British rear guard got frightened and retreated across the bridge. They went into position and fired. Hismer and Davis were killed, their words still in the air. The Minute Men shot back, killing three soldiers and wounding others. The British left for Boston, causing a running battle all the way back to Charleston Harbor. The Battle of Concord's North Bridge marks the first time colonists deliberately, and under orders from their commanders, fired on the British—it was treason.

## Greek Revival House
## East Willington, Connecticut

IT AMAZES ME that there are "Southern" houses in New England. Every New England town has white-columned, porticoed buildings. The Greek Revival style, which came into vogue around the 1820's, was obviously popular all over the country. The Building looks cold and hollow, you can hear the howling wind.

## First National Bank
## Fair Haven, Vermont

THE BANK FACES a town square full of autumn riot. The building is a crispy red and white, silhouetted against a cerulean fall sky.

70

## The State Capitol
## Montpelier, Vermont

COMPARED TO NEW Hampshire, Vermont looks poor—but it was beautiful, patterned in autumn. The State was an unknown wilderness until 1666, when a French officer established Ft. St. Anne. In 1724, Massachusetts colonists built Ft. Dummer (near Brattleboro). The French used forts at Chimney Point and Crown Point as bases for their attacks against the English from 1744 to 1759. In 1759, the French gave up their forts, and development was rapid.

Vermont was claimed by both New Hampshire and New York. In 1749, New Hampshire's governor began giving small land-grants. New York declared these void and tried to claim the grant monies. In 1770, the Green Mountain Boys were formed to protect the New Hampshire grants. Ethan Allen and those Green Mountain Boys captured Ft. Ticonderoga in 1775. In 1777, Vermont declared itself independent, and remained so for 14 years. In 1789, New York renounced its claims, and two years later, Vermont was admitted to the Union as the 14th state.

Montpelier is a tiny, pleasant town; it was chosen as the capitol in 1808. The capitol building was constructed in 1857. Its dome is made of wood covered with gold leaf. On top, and hiding in scaffolding, is Ceres, the Goddess of Agriculture.

71

## Mark Twain's House
## Hartford, Connecticut

I'M CONTINUALLY SURPRISED at the friendliness of the New Englanders. It was cold. I had to sit in a little arboretum, fern fronds dripping over my head, and peer through moss-frosted glass to glimpse Mark Twain's misplaced Mississippi steamboat. Mark Twain is one of my heroes; such an outrageous, outspoken, and honest person. I have even read that his books were once banned from the library shelves in Concord and Lexington.

The house he built bespeaks itself well of his own grandeur. It was designed by Edward Tuckerman Potter with the help of Twain and completed in 1874. Tiffany, in one of his earliest displays, created much of the interior decorative work. Mark Twain lived here from its completion until 1891. It was here that he wrote seven of his major works, including "Tom Sawyer" and "Huckleberry Finn." The house is strewn about with patterns: frumpy pillows made of oriental rugs; seats covered with Oriental rugs, and patterned rugs on top of patterned rugs on the floors. His workroom opened onto a balcony not unlike the bridge of a Mississippi paddle-boat. The front railing is a pilot's wheel. In the workroom is a giant billiard table on which Twain littered manuscript pages.

## "Wedding Cake House"
## Kennebunk, Maine

THE HOUSE WAS built in 1826 by George W. Bourne. Mr. Bourne is the present owner's great-great-grandfather. The house, though built of brick, was painted bright yellow so it would look like wood. Thirty years after its construction, Mr. Bourne (who obviously believed an idle hand is the Devil's workshop) added the fretwork. He carved each piece of wood by hand, and painted it white to look like stone. Every part of the house denies the concept of "truth to material."

Bourne, in his carvings, felt he was copying the Cathedral in Milan. The brick part of the building is in the Federal style. The cathedral drippings give the house the distinction of being classified as "an outstanding example of American-Domestic-Gothic Revival." It's often called the Wedding Cake House.

## The School Street Methodist Church
## Gorham, Maine

GORHAM WAS ONCE one of "those little New England towns." It still is, in many ways. But not for long—Portland is creeping in, and will soon make the place into a bedroom community. The independence (that the people fought to create and preserve) of the town, symbolized by the typical white-spired church, will be absorbed into the fabric of franchised-America.

Originally, Maine was part of Massachusetts, it became a State in 1820. It was through Maine that Colonel Benedict Arnold led the expedition to take Quebec. He and his men left on September 16, 1775, and returned, defeated, on the last day of December. Within the first week of the march, most of the food was spoiled, or lost in rivers and bogs. (It is difficult for us modern Americans to understand the primitive, 200 year-ago past.) The men had to eat their moccasins and their shot pouches. Hundreds died.

The first white man settled Gorham in 1736; by 1745 the town was incorporated. During the Revolution, men like the McLellans, Phinneys, Kellogs and Watems, whose families still live in the town, "did many brave and noble deeds."

# The Midwest

**City Hall and Astor Warehouse**
**Mackinac Island, Michigan**

## The Livestock Exchange
## Kansas City, Missouri

THE LIVESTOCK EXCHANGE Building looks like it should be engraved on the back of a twenty-dollar bill. It's such an American piece of architecture—not fancy, just matter-of-fact and to the point. This particular building was constructed in the early 1900's. This is the place where the farmers come to sell their cattle and to meet one another, discussing the day's problems in drawls and overalls. They're often dirty, and smell of manure, and they make a wonderful picture, sitting in the cafeteria/restaurant eatin' spinach and grits, and talking to the rough truck drivers.

## City Hall and Astor Warehouse
## Mackinac Island, Michigan

THERE ARE STILL a lot of ferries left. In Northern Michigan you can take a ferry up to Mackinac Island, a Victorian place with no cars. It is a quiet and spiffy place. The towered building (1839), was the original County Courthouse. The long structure was John Jacob Astor's fur warehouse (1817-1834). Michigan started here —Jean Nicolet visited the island and Lake Michigan in 1634. The first permanent settlement in the State was Sault Ste. Marie, founded by Fr. Marquette and Fr. Dablon.

## Tim Conley's House
## St. Louis, Missouri

LAFAYETTE SQUARE, ONCE the most elegant part of St. Louis, is where this house sits. Tim Conley lives here, and he is credited with creating, in 1969, Lafayette Square, Inc. It's the same year my friends and I created SOHO. I always thought it was just and proper that Tim and I should meet. The park that Tim's house faces, is the most beautiful and Victorian of any I've seen. People in modern clothes strolling under big old trees, the smell of the church barbecue down the street, the shouts of basketball players, somehow it all seems timeless. And beautiful.

This building was designed by George I. Barnett, and is part of a structure that dates back to 1843. The new structure was begun in 1850, and the 1876 Mansard roof was added. Montgomery Blair, for whom the house was built, was Postmaster for President Lincoln.

Though the area around Lafayette Square is a slum, it has fine old weathered-brick structures. All of St. Louis is fine, and old, and weathered. The downtown is rather a mess, but speckled with marvelous examples from every style of American architecture. Even now it is rumoured that more millionaires live in this city than anywhere except New York. St. Louis was the center of culture for the whole Mississippi Valley. In 1835, there were at least fifteen opera houses.

The famous arch isn't the Gateway to the West, it's the last fling of the East. Kansas city is the Gateway to the West. The sophistication that created St. Louis is decidedly a blend of those old traditions from the South and the Eastern seaboard. The people who made the city and got their money from it, left. They kept going further and further out, and by the 1940's, St. Louis was a rotten core, typical of most American urban areas. On the outskirts of this core, behind private gates and comfortable under the watchful eyes of old trees and uniformed guards, sit row upon row of grandiose mansions. Those areas aren't rotted at all.

Lafayette Square, too, has followed the path of the city, but it was the end of the Civil War and the influx of both Southerners and Europeans come to seek their fortunes that almost destroyed that place. When Tim Conley bought Blair House, there was one toilet under the staircase and sixty-two people stuffed into nooks and crannies. Now Lafayette Square is becoming an un-slum. Thank the Lord for Tim Conley.

## The Liberty Memorial
## Kansas City, Missouri

THE LIBERTY MEMORIAL is one of the most beautiful monuments I've found. It stands stark against Kansas City, a symbol of people who are proud and progressive. The monument was dedicated in 1921. At the dedication were 100,000 persons including Admiral Beatty, General Pershing, Vice President Calvin Coolidge, and the heads of State from Belgium, France, and Italy. The Memorial was designed by Howard Van Buren McDonagll.

The museum on the left is one of those run-of-the-mill war museums, but the right building, the Hall of Memory, is a stirring place. The interior is covered with murals that were started even before WWI was over. There are some amazing statistics: over one hundred artists worked on the north wall. There are at least six thousand portraits, and one of the world's largest paintings. The solemn message is hauntingly expressed by groups of plaques full of names. The plaques are labeled "We Are The Dead."

## Kemper Arena
## Kansas City, Missouri

OUTLANDISH THOUGH IT may appear, Kemper Arena follows the traditions of Kansas City. It is the new home of the Kansas City Kings and the American Royal, which is one of the country's finest livestock and horse expositions. A nice blending of tradition and newness. The Arena was honored in 1976 with a national award from the American Institute of Architects. It was cited for dramatic use of a supporting structure to produce a column-free interior, and is considered a dramatic and powerful architectural statement.

It almost floats like a blimp, swimming in a sky of asphalt parking lots. It's smart, but woefully alone in its black-topped setting. The architects were C.F. Murphy Associates, of Chicago. They put the thing together so cleverly, and so up to date, that the exterior steel trusses were easily dismantled for the Republican Convention in 1976 to move in more wiring and lighting-camera equipment.

## Masonic Temple
## Cass Avenue
## Detroit, Michigan

DETROIT'S LIBRARY SHOWS pictures of Cass Avenue that are so old there are wooden buildings all around. But my favorite pictures are those showing the area littered with grand mansions. Some of those mansions are still left: great brick piles, mansard roofs and towers jutting beyond the clutter and debris of modern Detroit.

This is the first time I've ever been intimate with such a place. Somehow, even with the filth, it seems magical. The Cass Avenue block, with The Bird Town Pet Shop and Aquarium, is typical. And through the strange yellow air the Detroiters call "haze," you can still breathe the street. It isn't too hard to imagine the whole area loaded with great townhouses. Now homes for people who have no place else. People are all over the stoops, sitting on railings, draped out windows. Dirty, tired, and somehow romantic. The 3400 block is like a time-study: a mansion being destroyed, a mansion still there; and an old house converted to a TV repair shop and straining at the change.

It's all like a bombed-out city. Maybe what London looked like after the War. So many wonderful old houses gutted; windows broken out, roofs caved in. Beautiful buildings. And only a few spots where those buildings are protected. (Detroit is well known for its lack of concern about things historic.) Oh, it is a mean place, that's for sure.

Yet, all isn't ugly. At one end of the Corridor is the Masonic Temple, a symbol of the '20's Renaissance and still the pride of Detroit. It

towers above the city around, a fairy tale cathedral.

And, at the other end, the prideful Fisher Building. Built at a cost of over $30,000,000, it is still a perfect monument. It soars to the tune of Detroit, singing the song of the greatness that is sometimes America. Not a song about tired street people; not a story of the down-and-out; but a song of hope. May it be a symbol for our future.

## 2031 Park Avenue
## St. Louis, Missouri

LINK, DESIGNER OF the St. Louis train station, designed this charming little townhouse for his brother, another Link. The building, which looks like a second cousin to the train station, sits facing wonderful Lafayette Square.

## The Fisher Building
## Detroit, Michigan

DETROIT IS SO car-oriented that drag queens wear blinking headlights on their chests. Leering as they dance, they are the perfect reflection of the Motor City.

The Fisher Building is the symbol of that city—it is the Fishers that are responsible for the designs of many American auto bodies. It is a towering monument, built in the late '20's in the most amazing Deco style. With all its grinning faces, it looks down on the freeways and the city. It is a beautiful building, and Detroiters are justly proud. Albert Kahn was the architect and the cost was $30,000,000.

The city was founded in 1701 by Antonine Cadillac (a headstrong, almost nasty, character)...in 1763 Pontiac tried to reclaim Detroit. All the industries' pioneers: Ford, Durant, Olds, Chrysler, and Buick—they all worked from Detroit. And they changed our lives; they changed the world.

## The Corn Palace
## Mitchell, South Dakota

SOUTH DAKOTA IS called "The Land of Infinite Variety." Looking at the Corn Palace, how can one doubt it?

In 1892, when Mitchell had only a 12-year history and 3,000 people, the World's only Corn Palace was established. L.O. Gale and Lewis E. Beckwith patterned the idea after a similar venture in Sioux City, Iowa which had failed to catch on. As has been true to the present, the building was redecorated each autumn with naturally coloured corn cut in halves and nailed up to make mosaics, with other grains and native grasses. Under the crazy spires such notables as John Philip Sousa and his Band, and Lawrence Welk, have entertained the people.

The Corn Palace is always different, and always wonderful. It is a living proof that architecture can be fun and a source of unique pride to a community. In the 1890's, the Palace and the Corn Belt Exposition existed "to lift the minds above the humdrum duties of life, and give play to the higher faculties of man."

Each year an artist creates new designs for the building. He first paints the various panels in miniature. Each panel is then laid out in full scale detailing in chalk on black roofing paper. The roofing paper is tacked to the large panels. The ears of corn are sawed on power saws, and nailed flat side to the panels. Hand axes are used to trim angles. Like a mosaic, each ear is considered for color and alignment. There are over 2,000 bushels of grasses, grains and corn used each year.

The current building, dedicated in 1921, was designed by George L. Rapp, of Chicago. There have been other Corn Palaces, each of them mad and glorious. It's a fine place, and the people of Mitchell are justly proud.

## Fort Abercrombie
## Fort Abercrombie, North Dakota

THE WIND WAS howling at fifty miles an hour. It was cold outside. Desolate. Did I hear people walking? No, there weren't any people. I was alone with the dreadful dust and the bending, barren trees.

Haunted Fort Abercrombie: a place authorized to be built in 1857 to protect the extensive trade between Canada and the North West, with St. Paul. The Fort is located near the Red River, in the Red River Valley.

84

## The Buell Building
## Rapid City, South Dakota

THE BUELL BUILDING is the soul of Rapid City. It stands rough and ready in that raw, new-feeling town. The city is fast becoming another tinsel and neon American place. This onion-domed old place only tenuously hangs on as a reminder of a more individualistic past.

No one is sure when the building was built, however it is documented from 1889. Charles J. Buell purchased the structure in 1901 and his son seems to remember that it was built by a Mr. Flormann. Early tenants were, the U.S. Land Office, the U.S. Weather Bureau, Mallow Meat Market, and the Gay Bump Bicycle Shop. Mrs. Clara Lobdell remembers getting her first permanent in Green's Beauty School, when it was in the Buell Building.

The town is folksy and sophisticated. Way out there in the Southwest part of the Midwest, the people are quite uptown. They were sophisticated in creating the Buell Building, and they're still sophisticated—a local restaurant currently features a French accented Maitre d' from Brooklyn.

## The Mitchell Building
## Milwaukee, Wisconsin

THIS IS A wonderful building, it was erected in 1876, by Alexander Mitchell. The whole city is wonderful, it reminded me of the Superman funny books from when I was a little boy. The downtown is loaded with fine buildings and interesting streets. There is even a river that runs through the city. I saw Paul Lynd, dashing about in a flowing caftan and loaded with jewelry, followed by an entourage of adoring fans. They zipped through the night streets in a Batmobile-like Cadillac—just like in a funny book.

It really is a nice place, Milwaukee, but I'd like to change the name to Gotham City.

## The Galloway House
## Fond Du Lac, Wisconsin

IN 1787, FOND Du Lac was a trading post. In 1819, the trading ended. By 1825, the trading post had been burned, and by 1832, the Winnebagoes and Patawatomis sold the land.

The Galloway House was started in 1848. The original small building was purchased by Edwin H. Galloway in 1868, from Selim Newton, and it began a transformation into a Midwestern Italianate Villa. Mr. Galloway Sr. died in 1876, but the house continued to be enlarged by his son, Edwin A. Galloway. Edwin P. Galloway donated the house and grounds to the Fond du Lac County Historical Society in 1954.

The building stands as a tribute to the American success story. The elder Galloway first lived in a shack, then a log cabin. Slowly he created the monument that stands today. It is a monument with 30 rooms, a twinkling music box, and the family dog—stuffed and comfortable—resting on the living room floor.

The house sits in a "village" of old things, sort of a preserve. Other buildings have been moved onto the Galloway land—permitting the lazy tourist a look at architectural styles that don't really belong together. It is such a pleasant place, that I can almost forgive the Historical Society for building fake structures—not entirely forgive but almost.

87

## View of the Murat
## Indianapolis, Indiana

THIS IS NOT a view of Istanbul. This is Indianapolis. They say the Midwest is bland. Well, obviously that's not true. The Midwest is an ersatz place, born of many peoples, reflective of many cultures. I find the area is quiet, introspective, and standoffish, and I also find it rather spectacular.

Brick tenements, a sleazy Sears and Roebuck shop, weeds and flapping laundry...and somewhere in that maze of bricks begins the mighty Murat. Indianapolis is a sometimes grand, sometimes a crummy, place. There is that old tragedy, the city destroyer called Urban Redevelopment. The pockets of remaining Indianapolis are worth a visit. The people are worth much more. They're nice there. They even walk up to you, knowing you're not a Hoosier, smiling and saying "welcome to our city."

Their temple (in which the concept of Shrine Children's Hospitals was born) was built in 1909. Oscar D. Bohlen was the architect, and was directed by Illustrious Potentate Elias J. Jacoby. An addition to the structure was dedicated in 1923. The name, Murat, remembers Bir Murat, an oasis in the Nubian desert. Marshall Murat was the General in charge of Napoleon's (1796-1800) army in Egypt. He was later the King of Naples. Murat always provided water for his soldiers.

## The Skyline
## Chicago, Illinois

IF AMERICA IS dying, as many people like to say, it is doing it in high style in Chicago. Such a marvelous city—I'd not ever seen anything like it. The people are friendly and the architecture is stimulating. It is a throbbing, growing place. And the wealth...from the city to the Wisconsin border...I have never seen so many huge mansions and sculptured gardens.

But the city...from my 18th floor view at Oak and Rush I could watch, I felt, the whole world. I saw people sitting and talking in old hotels. I saw new skyscrapers being constructed, people on street corners, cars rushing about. Just look: on the far left is the world's most expensive building, The Standard Oil Building. It's sheathed in marble. Next you can see a little piece of the Chicago Tribune, one of the world's great newspapers. On the other side of, and behind, the Maryland Hotel, is the Wrigley Chewing Gum Building—see that little dome? Next is the IBM Tower. At night it blinks, rows of lights cutting off and on, just like a machine. The circular scalloped buildings are the Marina Towers, with a fortress-like bank behind them. Behind the busy YMCA, is the world's tallest bureaucracy building, the Sears Tower. Beyond the "Y" is Joseph Kennedy's Merchandise Mart. It is a grand city. People chit-chat with you on elevators.

**110 East Mission Street
Strawberry Point, Iowa**

THE TALLEST BUILDING in Strawberry Point, Iowa, faces the road used in the great west-ward trek. This tower watched the pioneers as they wove their uncertain way.

**1120 Second Avenue
Cedar Rapids, Iowa**

**Tower Grove
Cedar Rapids, Iowa**

SOME PEOPLE SAY the Second Avenue House was built by the Worth Averil family in 1890. Other people say that construction began in 1870. Originally the third floor was a ballroom. The home was about to be bulldozed in 1974, when it was purchased for an Alcoholic Halfway House. ''Most everything here gets torn down.''

Tower Grove is considered a pre-Civil War structure, and is one of the favorite landmarks of Cedar Rapids. As history goes, the city is new. Its first settlers appeared in 1838; the town was chartered in 1849 and was thriving by the 1850's.

Grant Wood lived in Cedar Rapids. He painted those staunch and dreary people from his studio behind the local funeral parlor.

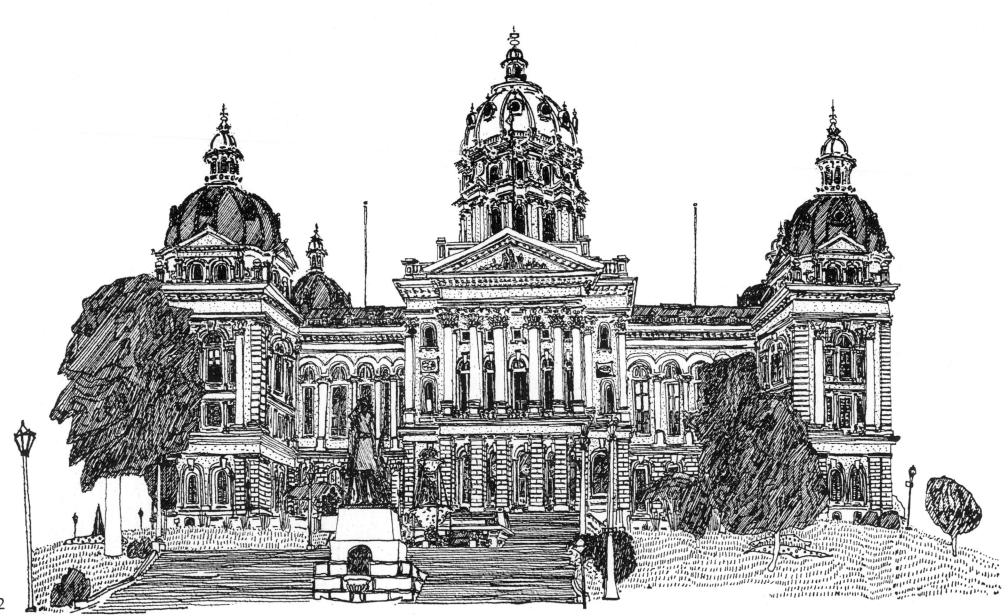

## The House Where Wyatt Earp Lived
## Pella, Iowa

IOWA COUNTRYSIDE IS lovely, a beautiful land, a state of diverse communities; Amish, Germans, and Dutch settled here. Their cultures are still in evidence. The first white men, Marquette and Jolliet, saw Iowa in 1673; the land became part of the United States in 1803, with the Louisiana Purchase.

The charming town of Pella was founded by H.P. Scholte and a group of religious refugees in 1847. Pella is a Dutch community—who would have ever guessed that Wyatt Earp spent his boyhood years in this simple 1850's building? The house was built by the Van Spankeren family. It was part home, and part General Store. The brick structure is now restored as a museum.

## The State Capitol
## Des Moines, Iowa

THIS IS A beautiful Capitol building, although now that I've seen most states, I think they're all kind of beautiful.

The Iowa State Capitol was dedicated in January of 1884 and is the pride of Des Moines. It seems a part of some book-ends, the other part being Terrace Hill, a Victorian piece being restored for a new Governor's Mansion. The two ends hold together another one of those confusing American urbanscapes: some fine old structures, the usual conglomerate of nonentity modern stuff, and millions of parking lots.

The design for the structure was created by architects Cochrane and Piqueard. "Architect Bell took over when Piqueard died."

I think of the structure as a monument to the vastness and strength of our great Midwest. The people of Iowa are not unlike their Capitol, aloof surely, but friendly and approachable if you take the effort to climb the steps.

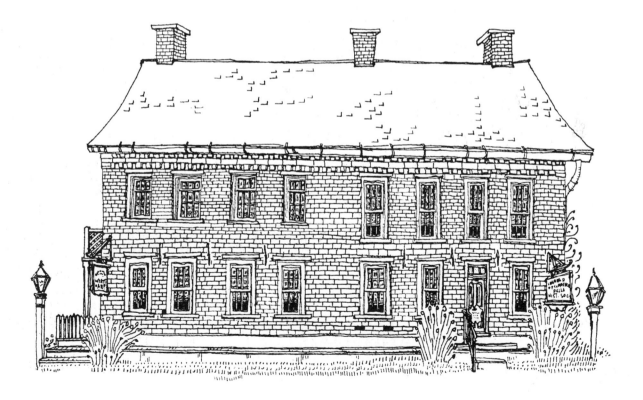

## The Dodge House
## Council Bluffs, Iowa

IOWANS THINK OF themselves as superior to their neighbors across the river in Nebraska. They are of an older culture, you know. And in Council Bluffs, the citizens proudly tell you that Lincoln's family owned land in the area until quite recently.

The Dodge House was designed by William Boyington, who also designed the Chicago Water Tower. It looks across the Missouri through the crispy fall sunshine. It peers at the new frontier and listens to the lonely sound of trains . . .an aristocratic structure, the home isn't much like its town. Council Bluffs (Lewis and Clark here held council with the Indians) city is a mess—crumbling old buildings, cut up by Urban Redevelopment and freeways leading one away as fast as possible.

General Dodge was a character and is called the greatest railroad builder of all times. He was also a statesman, a financier, and a friend of presidents. He came, with his bride, to Council Bluffs in 1854. Grenville Mellen Dodge came to town to make a railroad survey. The Civil War interrupted his business activities, but he persevered and became a Major-General. (A real Victorian codger, he was—persnickety and mean. They say he is responsible for the deaths of eighty men in Dodge City, Kansas—it was winter and he wouldn't let the soldiers build shelters. They froze.)

As befitting the owner of a grand mansion, General Dodge was president of sixteen companies, mostly having to do with the railroads. The train whistles moan of that glorious time

when General Dodge was friendly with Presidents Lincoln, Grant, Johnson, McKinley, Taft, and T. Roosevelt, not to mention those other rascals Carnegie, Vanderbilt, Gould, and Huntington.

94

## Dvorak's Summer House
## Bily Clock House
## Spillville, Iowa

IF YOU SIT, on a fall afternoon, in the little town of Spillville, you can hear music. I know that sounds ridiculous, but if you just sit quietly and look at the coloured leaves, and the little buildings, you can hear the sounds of Dvorak. Dvorak is famous for writing The New World Symphony; music that talks about America. But I'd never heard the "American Quartet" until recently, so that's why I came to Spillville.

Dvorak spent the summer of 1893 in Spillville. He came there at the suggestion of a student-friend. Spillville was a Czech town, and Dvorak felt the need to be with his fellow countrymen.

The name Spillville is actually appropriate. Dvorak's violins trip along like cold water running over rocks in the streambed. Spillville is

an Americanization of Spielville. Joseph Spielman located in this lovely spot in 1854 and a little town grew.

The building where Dvorak stayed is now a clock museum. Frank and Joseph Bily, natives of Spillville, are honored by their clock collection.

## Kinsman House and Office
## Warren, Ohio

WARREN IS BOTH beautiful—like all the little Ohio towns I've visited, and ugly—smokey and dirty—like the big cities. It is an old place, and was part of the Western Reserve, an area set aside and under the close watch of the founding fathers. Frederick Kinsman was an important part of the Reserve's history. The small building was Frederick Kinsman's office. It was built in 1822, when American architecture was fashionably Greek. People like Jefferson had studied the Greek philosophies, and those studies were carefully reflected in the architecture of the period. The main house, built in 1832, is also Greek Revival. It was created by the master builder, Isaac Ladd. The structure was altered and enlarged in 1846 and 1860.

## Theatre Center
## Oklahoma City, Oklahoma

OKLAHOMA IS A new State, admitted to the Union in 1907. The area was acquired as part of the Louisiana Purchase, and for a while, was designated Indian Territory. It was open to WASP settlement in 1889. There is a feeling of newness prevalent in Oklahoma City.

The Theatre Center is an outstanding example of the newness. When you see this place, you want to get out and walk around. Ramps beckon, corrugated walls wiggle; it's surely a fine place.

Most of Oklahoma City has been destroyed. They're trying to create an entirely new metropolis. I'm not sure how they're doing; it's rather confusing there, but if the people build more buildings like the Theatre Center, everything will be okay.

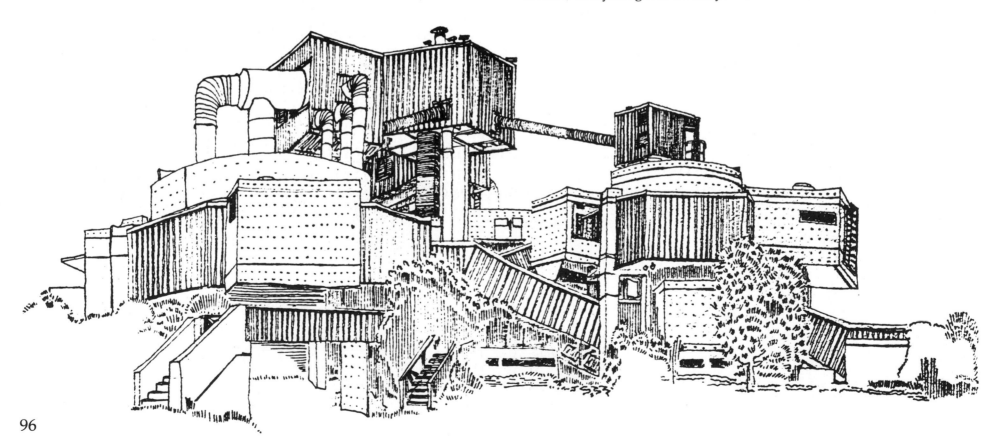

## House with Gargoyles
## Atchison, Kansas

I CAME TO Atchison because the name sounds like a place of pilgrimage. It's here, of course, that the Great Railroad started, and wound up in ancient Santa Fe. The town is loaded with fine buildings, and almost every one of them has a sign proudly proclaiming National Historic Sitedom. I'm sure this building is one of the most important in the city. It is locally known as the Devil's House. That's because of the gargoyles on the roof.

Local history has it that the man who lived here afforded his castle by selling his soul to the Devil. He got so rich that he was able to build another wonderful house next door (and across the street), and it was connected to his house by a tunnel. The second home was, of course, for his mistress. There are further histories whispered—satanic mysteries practiced under the Devil Shrines. And, do I remember something about Black Masses down in the tunnels? Now that's what I call History. Folk history it may be, but who knows? The house does seem spirited and menacing. One side has a balcony that looks like a gaping mouth, snapping out at unwary passers-by. Little carved creatures abound in the garden. No doubt they crawl about the facade, too.

97

## Nicolai's Farm
## Hampton, Minnesota

NOT FAR FROM the great metropolis of Minneapolis sprawls Nicolai's farm, a conglomeration of old barns and new barns, silos and pump houses. There's a broken windmill. And behind the great trees, a Victorian farmhouse. You pass a million places like this as you drive through Minnesota. There is a serenity: cows mooing and machinery clanking. I reckon this farm is really the American Dream. Space and peace, the comfort of self-sufficiency.

## Bud Olson's Bar
## Omaha, Nebraska

2622 LEAVENWORTH IS an historic structure, for it's this building that tells the real story of Omaha. Its tattered and pulled window shades whisper remembrances of stockyards, and a cowboy lifestyle. The Roman Catholic Church has bought up most of the neighborhood and has created an old-folks' highrise. Property values are escalating. At the same time there are problems and crime. Mr. Nemec had to close his drugstore. You see, he had so many things for sale that his windows were blocked with shelves. He got robbed all the time because no one could even see in. The barber-shop too has a For Rent sign. Bud's Bar is the major bit of life: inside those old soiled windows you can see the typical dyed-and-teased-haired Midwestern waitress serving ready-made sandwiches from one of those cook-em-in-an-instant machines. In the evenings the bar fills up with people I couldn't find anywhere else: like tough looking Indian girls with glossy black hair, slinging themselves onto chipped wooden tables and the Levi'd laps of their men friends.

# The West

**Pueblo
Taos, New Mexico**

## District Post Office
## San Antonio, Texas

I THOUGHT SAN Antonio was just the Alamo. It's not at all just that. There is a wonderful blending of old and new.

It feels bold and proud, like this 1891 building. It, as a city, is aware of what it has been, and doesn't intend to forget.

## Pueblo
## Taos, New Mexico

THE PUEBLO HAS stood in the same place, a little above the much later town of Taos, for fifteen hundred years. The pueblo looks today, much the same as it always has, strong and silent; a protection against the cold winter winds and the heat of summer. It is the first real American architecture. It has a direct influence on modern American architecture.

102

## The Bishop's Palace
## Galveston, Texas

THE PALACE WAS built by Col. Gresham and his wife for themselves and their nine children. Col. Gresham was involved in everything: cotton, shipping, the Texas Legislature, and the Federal Congress. They were also rich; they travelled all over the world to furnish their 1880's mansion. The cost was $250,000 and it took six years to build. In 1923 Mrs. Gresham sold the building to the Roman Catholics.

Each room is unique, being designed around fireplaces. The walls are 23 inches thick, the mirrors are from France, the parlour is done in a silk brocade from London, and the shutters are hand-made and some have silver hinges. Nicholas Joseph Clayton was the architect, he designed the building when he was 35. He is the first really well-known architect in Texas. Mrs. Gresham loved lillies and children's faces. Both are painted on canvases and designed into the jeweled stained glass. The children's faces are Greshams—with the addition of angelic wings. One of the strangest things in the house is the grand player piano in the music room. A guide turns on a button, (the house was electrified when it was built) the keys dance up and down, music fills the rooms and echoes all over the mansion. There is something especially vibrant about the sound. It is "Rhapsody in Blue." Gresham himself is playing.

103

## Barrio Apartment
## El Paso, Texas

EL PASO SITS at the end of the Rockies. It is one of only two natural passes through the mountains. The original town was Juarez (a part of Mexico) and was called "El Paseo del Norte." It is a town that is now rushing into the modern world. There are many new buildings, none of which relate to the strange surrounding desert.

Down by the border are still streets lined with Mexicanesque brick buildings; full of life.

104

## The Old Cotton Exchange
## Houston, Texas

THIS IS A funny looking building now, but imagine what it looked like in 1884, when there was a bale of metal cotton rotating from a spindle in the center of the roof. The main door used to be in the center and lead into a grand hall. The hall had hand painted ceilings with cotton balls and vines twining about. Now the door is over to the left. Top storey is an addition. In 1907 a new floor was added, the cornice top was simply lifted higher. It was designed by Eugene T. Heiner. The building is called Victorian Rennaissance Revival—which just means it is a bit crazy.

## The Russian Orthodox Cathedral
## Sitka, Alaska

ST. MICHAEL'S CATHEDRAL was built by Bishop Innocent between 1848-50. The Cathedral was destroyed by fire in 1966 and has since been reconstructed.

Inside the rather rustic structure one finds Armstrong linoleum tiles and indoor-outdoor carpeting. The Sanctuary is almost tacky. But the golden appurtenances and heavy incense made me forget I was in a new place. Tlingit priests and a small congregation chant and bow and cross themselves in the old Orthodox manner. They seem to be struggling to continue a religion that deserted them after Russia sold the land to America.

## Painted Horn Trading Post
## Bluff, Utah

TRADING POSTS HAVE everything. Inside this one you can find somber-faced Indians trading jewelry, and blankets that they've woven in their dusty hogans. They drive up in shiny trucks full of their wares, and they leave with, sometimes groceries, sometimes money, sometimes perhaps, a new gun.

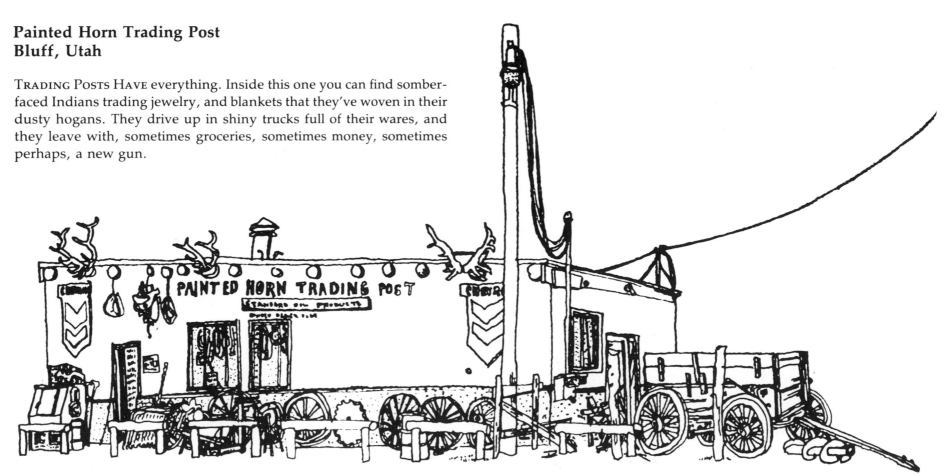

## The Temple
## Salt Lake City, Utah

ON JULY 28, 1847, Brigham Young put down his cane and said, "Here's where the temple will be built." That was before any structure had appeared in Salt Lake City. Construction began in 1853 and wasn't completed until 1893. The castle-like structure was made of granite which was hauled by oxen from a quarry 20 miles away. It's a magic feeling place, especially at night—all spires and lights, like a fairy tale palace.

107

## The Church
## Green River, Utah

GREEN RIVER HAS a different look. (It is the only town in Utah founded by people other than Mormons.) It's that dry, dusty-weather look. And the most dominant building in the town is the church. There is no cross on top.

108

## Cane House
## Lahaina, Maui, Hawaii

MAUI IS FAST becoming Hawaii's most popular Island. The Maui-mecca is a threat to these frame houses smothered by plants and strange trees. They are called Cane houses, because they sit in the sugar cane fields, and are lived in by the people who tend the fields. This particular house is home to a Filipino family that tends gamecocks. All day, and most of the night, you can hear the cocks crowing.

## The Palace
## Honolulu, Hawaii

THE IOLANI PALACE in Honolulu is the only Royal Palace in America. It was built for King Kalakaua, and Hawaiian Royalty ruled here from 1882 until the monarchy was overthrown in 1893. The building, European in design, replaced an earlier, simpler palace. Until 1968, Iolani Palace served as the Hawaiian State Capitol. It is presently undergoing restoration and will eventually be a museum.

## Molly Brown's House
## Denver, Colorado

MOLLY, A SIMPLE girl from Missouri, met J.J. Brown, a Pennsylvanian, in Leadville, Colorado. They married in 1886. They were rich, their money came from the Lucky Johnny, one of the many Leadville mines. In 1894 the couple moved to Denver and, to properly display their wealth, purchased this structure. The mansion was designed by William Lang of Denver for Isaac Large (another silver magnate).

The Browns didn't stay happily married. They separated in 1909 and Molly kept the house. Rumour has it that Denver society never quite accepted the lady.

A man on the street told me, "Molly warn't no good. She paid off the police and the government. They just gloss over all that. You ask the old timers around here."

Molly Brown achieved fame from the Titanic disaster of 1912, in Lifeboat #6. Molly saved waterlogged souls as the ship sank. It took that disaster to make Molly acceptable in 110 Denver.

## Davy's View Going into Telluride
## Telluride, Colorado

DRIVING INTO TELLURIDE, on the right are dreadful condominiums. On the left side is ancient and lovely Colorado. The structures are the remains of Colorado's first brewery, and the mountains, those wonderful strange mountains, are honeycombed with mines. In town one meets progressive young people— business oriented—and miners too. They're rough men, their talk is loaded with stories of the "underground."

## St. Nicholas Russian Orthodox Church
## Juneau, Alaska

LEFT OVER FROM an earlier time is the St. Nicholas Russian Orthodox Church (built in 1894). It is the oldest Russian church in Southeastern Alaska. The older parts of Juneau are similar to the church; quaint buildings jumbled onto windy streets and hanging from giant hills.

111

## View from 12th Street West
## Leadville, Colorado

LEADVILLE IS THE highest city in the United States, almost two miles above sea level. I don't know how many people live there because in Colorado they don't write populations on their signs, they just write elevations. The town became famous for its gold as early as 1860. In the ten year period between 1879 and 1889 $136,000,000 in ore was mined from the surrounding hills. The main street is rinky-tinky—it's easy to see the past. The little houses jumble together like a playing card village. The buildings are mostly of raw wood, echoing a rough and tumble culture and a cold and forlorn climate.

## Colorado Street View
## Telluride, Colorado

TELLURIDE HAS BEEN a secret town. No one had ever heard of the place, but now it is being billed as the new Aspen. Mining is real here. People talk about the mines when night comes. They sit in the bars drinking, and telling stories about what goes on down under. This is "Marlboro Country."

In 1878 the town was named Columbia, but it turned out that name had already been used somewhere else. Tellurium gold ore was mined in the area, so in 1882 the name was changed to Telluride. In 1897 there were a score of producing mines. By 1909, 60 million dollars in gold, silver, lead, and copper had been taken from the 340 miles of tunnels in the area. The past is full of tales and legends. Lillian Russell visited the town as did William Jennings Bryan. It was from the Sheridan Hotel (the brick structure second from the left) that Mr. Bryan made his "Cross of Gold" speech July 4, 1903. The Sheridan was built in 1897 by Brickson & Hippler. The walls, covered in calfskin, were an elegant addition to the young city. The Sheridan's still the place to go for an afternoon beer.

On the far left is the San Miguel County Courthouse. It was built in 1887. The stone building, now the Elks Lodge, was constructed in 1892 as the Mohr Building. In 1899 it became the San Miguel National Bank. The bank achieved its greatest fame when it was visited by Tom McCarty, Matt Warner, and George Leroy Parker. The three fellows withdrew $10,500 without benefit of an account, launching Parker on a career that made him one of America's folk heroes. (He changed his name to Butch Cassidy.)

113

## The Old Iron Front Building
## On N. Last Chance Gulch
## Helena, Montana

THE LOCALS CALL this The Iron Front Building. It was completed in 1887 at a cost of $100,000. The cast iron parts of the Templeton Hotel were made in Helena, and it's perhaps the only cast iron building in Montana. The formal and balanced style was derived from Italian Renaissance forms. Components for the building were manufactured by the John Stedman Foundry. In the '80's it was described as... "solid and substantial, as well as elegant and graceful in its apportionment."

## The Red Onion
## Aspen, Colorado

OUT IN COLORADO where women are haybags, and trucks are rigs, there are lots of saloons. The Red Onion is a typical bar. The structure remains as it was in 1892. Tom Latta, the original owner, catered to the sportin' men, and his saloon and gambling hall flourished. In good Western tradition, there was a whorehouse upstairs. They were still riding horses into the bar up until ten years ago.

## Copper Queen Hotel
## Bisbee, Arizona

THE COPPER QUEEN Hotel was built in 1904. It was considered to be the finest hotel between Los Angeles and El Paso. It has some of the finest food between Los Angeles and El Paso.

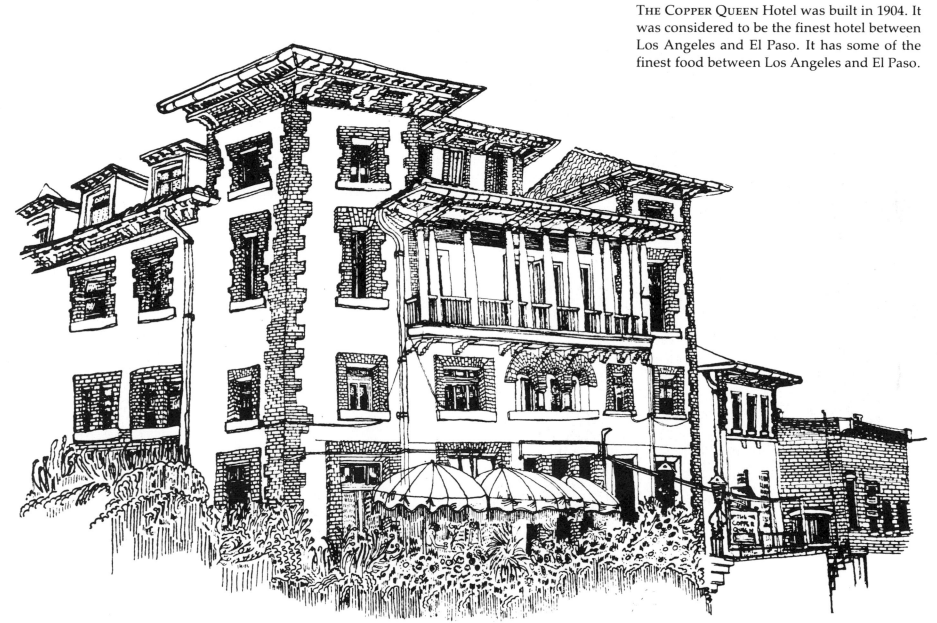

## South Pass City Ghost Town
## South Pass City, Wyoming

## The Carissa Mine
## Between South Pass City &
## Atlantic City, Wyoming

LONG PAST 1849 and the California Gold Rush, and long past the Oregon Trail (which meandered close by South Pass City), came the opening, in 1867, of the Carissa Lode. That peculiar, centipede-like mine crawled and clawed its way over the low hills, ignoring the lonely howling wind and the swift moving Wyoming clouds. The mine spewed gold, and the gold built those twin towns, Atlantic City and South Pass City. South Pass City possessed six general stores, three butcher shops, restaurants, and sawmills. Locals could purchase ready-made clothes in specialty shops and spend their golden profits at a jewelry store and a furrier's shop. Visitors had a choice of five Hotels. They could wash the dust out of their gullets at seventeen saloons. And there were lots of sportin' houses. Of course there were also blacksmiths, livery stables, and even a dentist. And this is all that's left.

## Street Scene
## Bisbee, Arizona

BISBEE IS A town of arid hills, covered with swaying and leaning old buildings. The Bisbee Copper mines built the town. Parts of the mine are closing and people are moving away. It is now said that "Aspen Money" is moving in and buying up everything. If you hurry there you can still see a mining town on the skids, rinky-tinky and real. Buildings like the towered Python Castle, built in 1903, ask that you stay a bit longer—take a little walk, feel a town unspoiled by the sameness of our modern world.

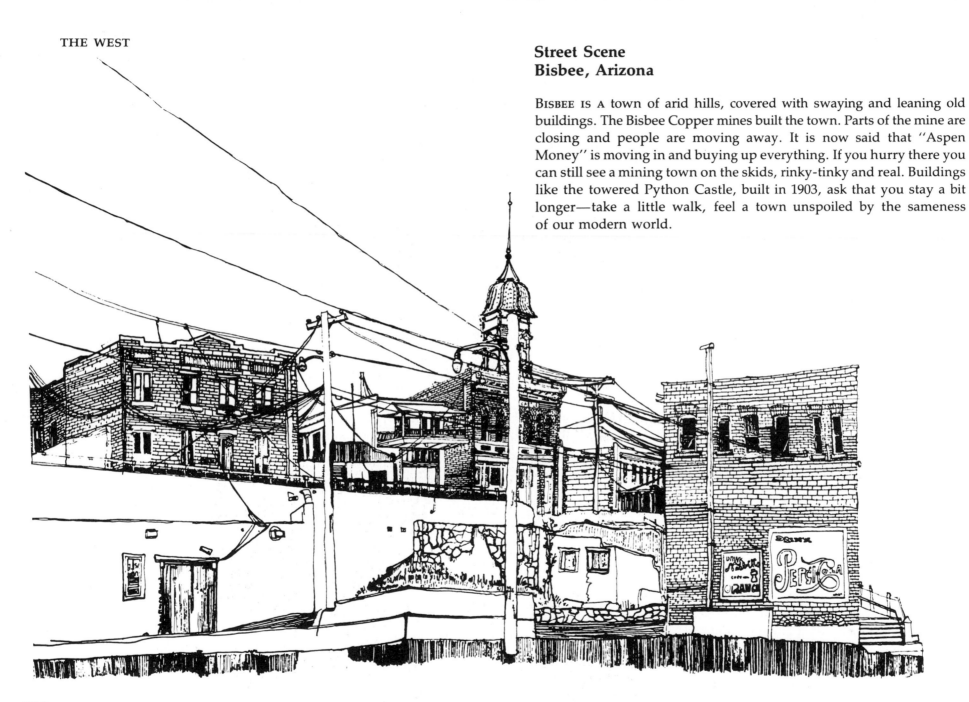

118

## The Curtiss Music Hall
## Butte, Montana

IMAGINE A MAN coming to this city and building a structure like this in 1892. Mr. Curtiss named his towering castle after himself—the Curtiss Music Hall. Curtiss brought the first player pianos to the Northwest, and used the first floor for the sale of those pianos and other musical instruments.

There was once a wrought iron balcony framing the third level. That's gone now. So are the miners who rented upstairs rooms. The rooms were rented in shifts to three people. One fellow would be in the mines for eight hours, one would sleep for eight hours, and the third miner would be left to his own devices on the streets. The first floor is still a viable part of Butte's urban culture. Gamer's Tea Room is a popular spot for afternoon meetings and snacks.

119

## The Boca House
## Socorro, New Mexico

THE BOCAS WERE a Spanish land-grant family in this isolated place. Socorro was once an important mining center. It was also the Territorial Capitol of New Mexico, with a population of 25,000. Now there are 5,000 people and the town looks asleep, like this 1885 hostelry.

It hasn't yet been gutted by urban redevelopment; there are trees, and old junky adobes, and a plaza. The plaza enshrines a piece of the original Atomic Bomb. The bomb was exploded only 50 miles from Socorro, continuing the violent nature of the land. There was Kit Carson rounding up the Indians, forcing them into corrals for people (and we call him a hero now), there was Billy the Kid, Pat Garrett, the Sundance Kid—they all saw Socorro.

## Bishop Rhea House
## Boise, Idaho

THE BISHOP'S HOUSE was built on land acquired in 1867. The Reverend Daniel S. Tuttle, the first Episcopal Bishop of Idaho, bought the whole block for $325. (It cost more than that to put a fence around the block.) Buffalo Bill was a visitor here; so was Marion Anderson.

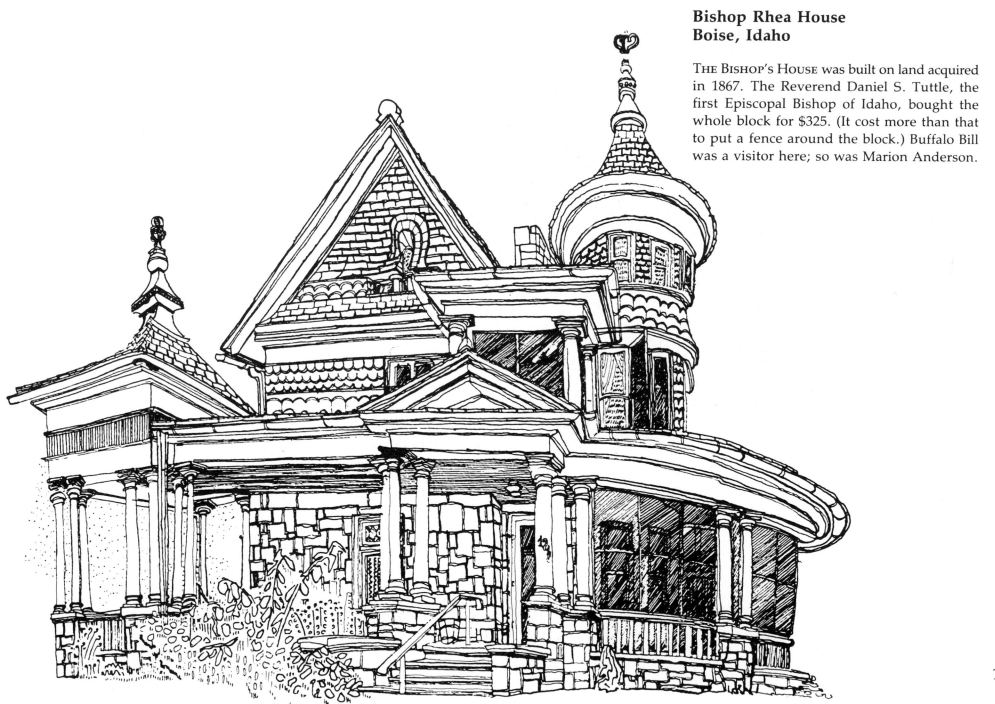

**Valdez House
Albuquerque, New Mexico**

THE HOUSE, ONE of the oldest structures in the city, once belonged to
an early Albuquerque family. It sits facing Old Town Square, and is an
integral part of the Mexican town.

## Main Street
## Nevada City, California

NEVADA CITY IS Disneyland come to real life. All these buildings look dreadfully cute and yet they are more than that. The people, the Gold Rush people, had eyes and minds that liked that sort of architecture. They look like toys. Most of the buildings were built in the 1850's, no later than the 1860's. One third of Nevada City's structures were lost to a freeway, and, even so, it is a spectacular place.

## The Vedanta Society Temple
## San Francisco, California

THE VEDANTA SOCIETY Temple was designed (after the Earthquake/Fire) by a swami and Joseph A. Leonard. It is the perfect San Francisco statement: a conscious blending of architectural styles; Hindu, English, Moorish, Mongol, Gothic, Byzantine—to teach that all religions lead to the same Unity. Eccentricity was expected, and still is expected in San Francisco.

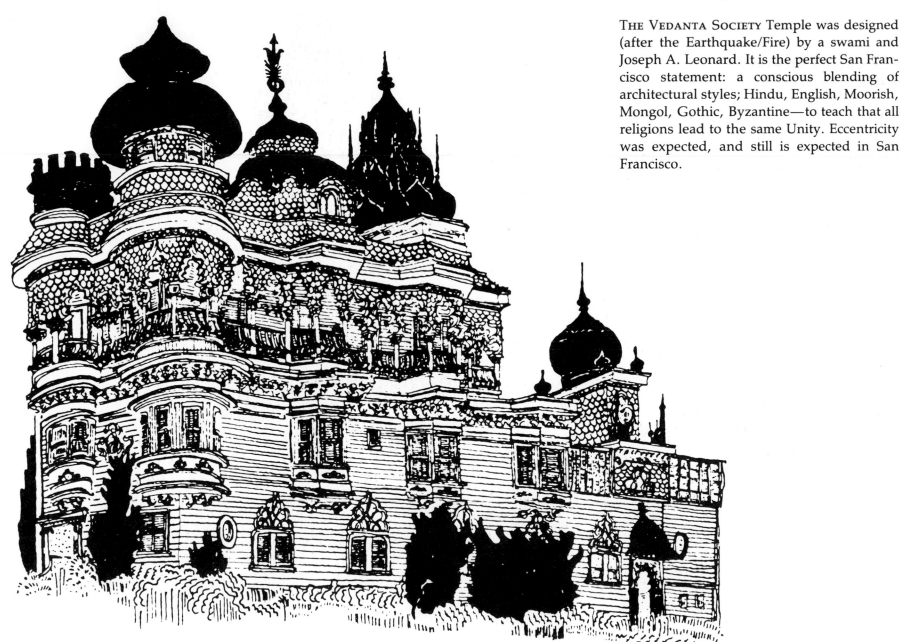

## The Carson Mansion
## Eureka, California

I WONDER IF this isn't the grandest Victorian house of them all. It is hard to believe that the kind of person who would build such a building wasn't laughing all the time. It's rich and wonderful and quite crazy.

Mr. Carson came to the Eureka area in 1850, determined to get in on the gold rush. But, he found that it was easier to work with lumber; he is credited with being the first person to mill a redwood. This building is redwood, most of California's Victorian buildings are redwood. Mr. Carson was responsible for the "beginning of the end" of the redwood forests, and he is responsible for this marvelous heritage of buildings. He was an ordinary man, he had ordinary tastes. Redwood made him a king, and as a king he seemed to develop capacities that were truly royal—look at his palace. When he died, in 1912, the whole town closed up for a day. Everyone loved him.

The 18 room mansion was built between 1884 and 1886. Carson's lumber mill workers were able to continue working through the depression of '85-'86, they simply worked on the Carson House. There were even two full-time wood carvers. Three generations of Carsons lived in the mansion. It was sold, in 1950, to a group of Eureka businessmen. The cost was $35,000 and the stipulation was that the home remain in its original state.

125

## Montgomery Street View
## San Francisco, California

SOME PEOPLE HERE are disgusted by the Trans-American Building. Perhaps it is true that San Francisco's most important tradition is to play a thing to the hilt. Almost everything in this view is unique, the site of California's first Masonic Temple, the West Coast headquarters for the National Trust for Historic Preservation, and Melvin Belli's office. On the right is the site of the first Jewish Temple in California.

In the tops of these big buildings, people do all sorts of commercial things. You can see the Wells Fargo Bank, the World Headquarters for the Bank of America...all those money palaces. Down around the bottoms are the famous shops; expensive clothing stores, architect's offices, designers' studios, fabric shops, and all the beautiful antiques in the world.

126

## House at Seminary and Third
## Napa, California

HERE'S WHAT MAKES a Victorian house! This building is a good example of a structure designed for living. A porch is a nice thing; it's a transition area between the outside world and the inside world. If you're sitting there in your rocking chair, talking with a friend, and you get bored, your eye can fly up and look at the shapes of the spools that pretend like they hold up the roof. If your eye travels down, you can wander through carved capitals. The columns themselves are almost giant spools. They sit on yet another decorative piece which throws out an entirely different spool.

Look at the walls; notice all the different "wall treatments." There's a nice cut-out pattern to start with, above that a railing, then a whole level of straight lines. But the wall doesn't do what we've been taught a wall is supposed to do. It doesn't meet with another wall at the proper ninety degree angle. Instead, it chops itself off and an inverted bay window is created. The same flag design that starts the first floor pattern, seems repeated in a flying overhang. Windows and doors make obviously interesting shapes. I happen to know that it's very nice to stand in a window like any one of these, and frame yourself.

Look at the second storey. Look what they dared to do in those inverted bay windows: spool work, spool columns, doughnut twists leaning out against the columns, and capitals suggesting the first level bannisters. Coloured glass appears in the windows—that's always nice to look through. Have you ever looked through a rose-coloured window? There are angles and patterns, constant variation; in fact, constant change as the shadows move through the day. Now that I think of it, a building like this really reflects the way life is—rather mad. And the whole building, this whole philosophical statement, seems whimsically, perhaps naively, reaching up. The finials do it.

127

## House With a Tower
## Petaluma, California

THE WRIST-WRESTLING Championships are held in Petaluma, California, and Petaluma is the chicken raising capitol of the world. It's the city that initiated policies to control wanton growth. The townfolk were not interested in becoming a Bay Area suburb. San Francisco is fine, they feel, but then so is Petaluma.

## Hermosa Vista
## Redlands, California

IF YOU EVER do a tourist thing in your whole life, it should be to come see this building. It's right near the Redlands Hospital. The house is named Hermosa Vista and was built in 1890. A Mr. Morey designed the house for himself and his family (with a little help from his friend, Mr. Seymour, a lumber man). Mr. Morey had been a shipwright and he applied boat-building techniques to the onion dome. Redlands is loaded with Victorian houses—it was quite a fashionable place to live in the '80's and '90's. It still is, I think.

## The Old Governor's Mansion
## Sacramento, California

BUILT IN 1877 for Albert Gallatin, the building, with its curved Mansard roof-line, was the first official California Governor's Mansion. Governor George C. Pardee moved there in 1903, and was the first of 13 governors to live in this marvelous house. Governor Ronald Reagan ended the 64 year tradition. The mansion is a symbol of what Sacramento was— the town seemed a magic square of dripping green trees, classic government structures, commercial buildings, and wonderful Victorian houses.

129

## Pan Pacific Auditorium
## Los Angeles, California

LOS ANGELES IS the home of the Glittered-Out-Rocky-Horror-Show-People. The exciting thing is, you don't know what's real. Neither do the people who live there. But that doesn't matter. It is all done for style. That's what is real there; style.

Just look at the Pan Pacific Auditorium, it is space fantasy, pure space fantasy, future architecture. The sides are like two boats coming into a dock. The center is like four Godzilla claws mechanically waving in the yellow Los Angeles sky. The whole effect is a rocket-ship blasting off for some Buck Rogers planet.

## Cucamonga Community Methodist Church
## Cucamonga, California

"ALL ABOARD FOR Anaheim, Azusa, and Cuuuuucamonga." Now I don't know why anybody would go to Cucamonga, except the name is wonderful. The place is one of those Southern California leftovers, warmed up in the oven, it's still tasty, but sitting on a shelf, the town looks pretty dreary. The area was originally inhabited by some Indians. Then there was the time of the Silver Dons, and the valley breathed a romance as thick as its present day smog. Gringos came and the Mexicans lost control. Ranching, citrus and grapes became a lifestyle. This old stone church was built around 1909, and records mention 337 wagon loads of rocks brought down from the beautiful nearby mountains.

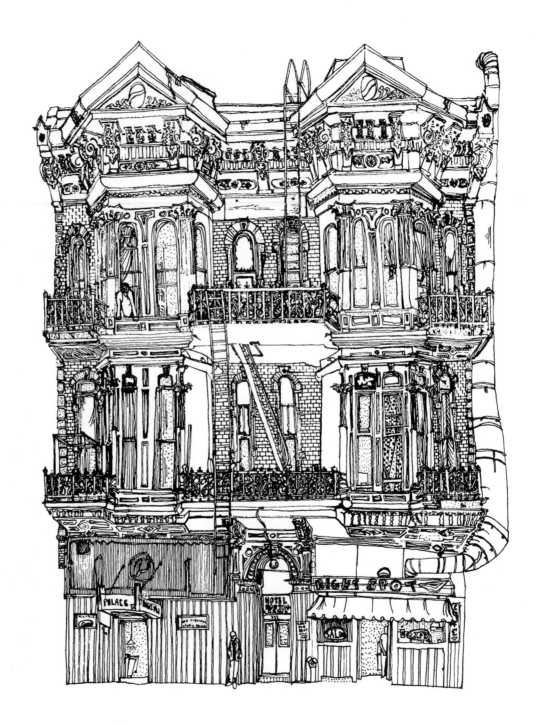

## The Horton Hotel
## San Diego, California

THE HORTON HOTEL sings a song. Some people, if they can hear the song at all, hear a song of the past—times gone by. But if you really listen, you hear a timeless song; horses clopping on dirt streets, buses roaring and sputtering; cowboys with six-shooters, blacks in flashy glitter. It is the song of San Diego—new and old. San Diego, raw city, fresh and wiggly, stretching and bending in silver morning fog, twisting to catch afternoon sunshine.

For me, the Horton Hotel is a symbol of San Diego, and it should live forever.

## Apartment Building with Towers and a "P"
## Los Angeles, California

LOS ANGELES—SOME people say it's a fake. But it isn't. Where else can you live in a castle, near the heart of one of the largest cities in the world?

Los Angeles is crazy: it is exciting. Off every freeway ramp is a world. It might be Chicano-decorated buildings shouting out vivid colour messages to the smogging traffic. It might be a fairy castle. It might be a tree-shrouded Victorian left-over, or it might be giant columns in the air—modern structures full of modern people.

Los Angeles dares to be a million different things.

133

## Bush House
## Salem, Oregon

THE BUSH HOUSE was built in 1877. Mr. Bush came to Oregon from Massachusetts and started a newspaper, "The Oregon Statesman." Later, as one of Salem's leading citizens, he started the Ladd & Bush Bank.

The house is a large and pleasant building, with lots of rooms and ten fireplaces. The fireplaces, as well as much of the furniture, came around the Horn. There is still a great deal of Bush furniture, and you can still see the original wallpaper. In the library the wallpaper has a marvelous Greek freize—the paper in each room is unique.

Bush lived in the house with his children and three servants. There is a shrine in the form of an after-death portrait of his wife. One can feel the presence of the dead woman everywhere. She never lived there.

The family lived in the house until 1953. At that time interested citizens began the movement which later resulted in the Bush House Museum. The house sits on 100 acres (Bush Meadows) and is the pride of Salem.

134

## The Pioneer Building
## Seattle, Washington

SEATTLE IS A big, sophisticated city, a beautiful setting with great old buildings. One whole section of the down-town is in the process of being preserved. At night the area is full of strollers, the rich folk visiting great restaurants (the Brasserie Pittsburg has been in this building since 1893), good music, even the slum dwellers left over from the old days. It is good to see a part of a city alive after 5 p.m.

The current restoration project is the Pioneer Building, in the legislatively-protected Pioneer Square. $2 million is being spent to refurbish this giant Romanesque Revival building. Henry Yesler, a Seattle pioneer who bought the first steam operated sawmill to Puget Sound, built the structure in 1892. During the Alaskan gold rush there were 48 gold mining firms housed here. On one side, in an alley, one can still see stubs of I-beams from the city's earliest "sky bridge" which carried the businessmen across to a hotel where they kept their mistresses. During prohibition the sixth floor of the building had a classy speakeasy. On the same site, in 1872, Henry Yesler donated the timbers which were stretched across some trees; a mob hanged three men from those timbers. Seattle is proud of the Pioneer Building.

## St. Paul's Episcopal Church
## Virginia City, Nevada

VIRGINIA CITY (called the city that built San Francisco) kept the United States solvent during the Civil War. The money from the silver mines made Nevada a state. Riches from the comstock Lode came to almost three quarters of a billion dollars. By 1863, the first Bonanza Period was going strong and by 1879, everything was over.

What a gentle building. There is a fragrance of spring flowers sitting on an old altar. This church was built in 1876, one of many structures still standing in Virginia City. The town is a bit rinky-tink now, I'll bet it felt the same way when silver and gold were being pulled from the surrounding hills. Even Mark Twain worked in Virginia City, and he was probably entertained at the opera house.

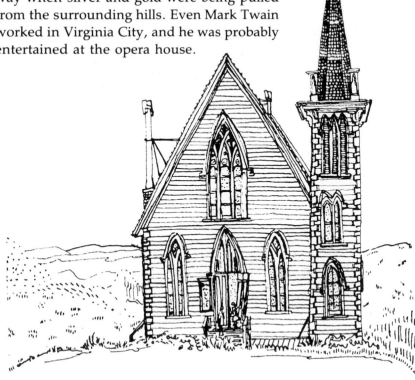

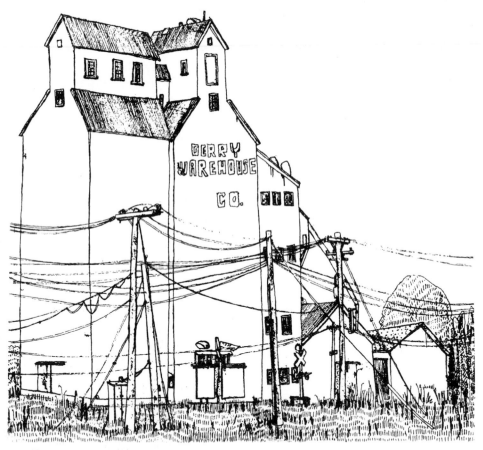

## Gerry Warehouse
## Richreall, Oregon

WAREHOUSE BUILDINGS LIKE this one, their accompanying railroad apparatus, and even the telephone lines, are an American monument.

## The Cavalier Motel
## Carlin, Nevada

WHEN WE THINK about America, we tend not to think of its ugliness. We forget that perhaps the majority of our buildings—our real living structures—are ugly things. Through the tumbleweeds and trash, this is a view of telephone wires streaking across the desert sky, great trucks zooming along the straight highway. Such desolation, such emptiness.

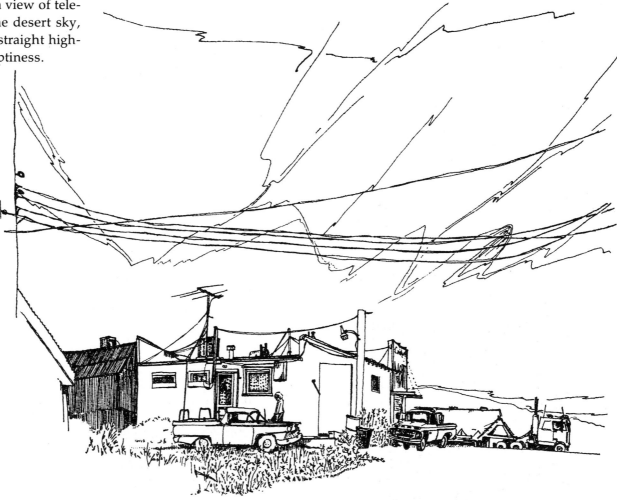

# The Collectors

The Horton Hotel
San Diego, California
Dale T. Craig

Pan-Pacific Auditorium
Los Angeles, California
Mr. & Mrs. E.C. DeClue

Apartment Building with a ''P''
Los Angeles, California
Peter A. McNames

Hermosa Vista
Redlands, California
Mr. & Mrs Glenn E. Murdock

Montgomery Street View
San Francisco, California
Ronald L. Wicks

The Vedanta Society Temple
San Francisco, California
Pat Hyndman

House With A Tower
Petaluma, California
David Allen

House at Seminary & Third
Napa, California
Mr. & Mrs. Joe R. Sutter

The Old Governor's Mansion
Sacramento, California
Claudia Mandell

Main Street
Nevada City, California
Peggy Jean McCarroll

St. Paul's Episcopal Church
Virginia City, Nevada
Richard Dart

The Carson Mansion
Eureka, California
Peter A. McNames

Bush House
Salem, Oregon
John A. Recht, D.V.M.

The Pioneer Building
Seattle, Washington
Peter A. McNames

The Bishop Rhea House
Boise, Idaho
Mr. & Mrs. Bobby Schwartz

The Church
Green River, Utah
Camille Currier

Painted Horn Trading Post
Bluff, Utah
Curly Wallace

Taos, West Pueblo
Taos Pueblo, New Mexico
Mr. & Mrs. Charles H. Johnson

Valdez House (Old Town)
Albuquerque, New Mexico
Mr. & Mrs. Richard S. Ybarra

The Boca House
Socorro, New Mexico
Mr. & Mrs. Bobby Schwartz

Barrio Apartment
El Paso, Texas
Mr. & Mrs. Bobby Schwartz

The Copper Queen Hotel
Bisbee, Arizona
Mr. & Mrs. Steve Hutchenson

Street Scene
Bisbee, Arizona
Gene Burkhard

Cane Houses
Lahaina, Maui, Hawaii
Alison Markel

The Bishop's Palace
Galveston, Texas
Ronald L. Wicks

Johnson's Press Shop
New Orleans, Louisiana
Hugh G. Grambaugh

D'Evereaux
Natchez, Mississippi
Gary Rees

The First Presbyterian Church
Port Gibson, Mississippi
Patrick Michael Gallagher

Corner of Church St. & Cedar St.
Mobile, Alabama
Reese LaRiviere

The Windsor Hotel
Americus, Georgia
Peter A. McNames

The Don Ces Sar Hotel
St. Petersburg, Florida
Clinton Wilder

Ca'd Zan
Sarasota, Florida
A.J. (Fred) Acheson

The Fontainebleau (Front View)
Miami Beach, Florida
Bruce Kay

Flagler College
St. Augustine, Florida
Mr. & Mrs. Rick Ybarra

New Hanover County Courthouse
Wilmington, North Carolina
Sue Cooper & John Alan Cooper

Bodie Island Lighthouse (Outer Banks)
Bodie Island, North Carolina
Ronald L. Wicks

Pembrook Avenue
Norfolk, Virginia
Bob Brown

Freemason Street
Norfolk, Virginia
Mary Parker Stuart

The Masonic Temple
Detroit, Michigan
Eugene Pettis

Cass Avenue, The Mugging
Detroit, Michigan
Ed Zerwekh

The Fisher Building
Detroit, Michigan
George Murphy

The Galloway House
Fond-du-Lac, Wisconsin
Michael D. Main

View From Ken's Window, #2
Chicago, Illinois
Mr. & Mrs. Rick Ybarra

Peter Hurdic Mansard
Williamsport, Pennsylvania
Wayne Fabert

The Stroud Mansion
Stroudsberg, Pennsylvania
Donald Mitchell, O.D.

Greenwich Village
New York City, New York
Michael Wayne Sullivan

School Street Methodist Church
Gorham, Maine
Edna Kamerling

Ash Street School
Manchester, New Hampshire
Linda Bonham

The Grist Mill
Ashland, New Hampshire
Mr. & Mrs. Kenneth L. Horstmann

The Homestead
Sugar Hill, New Hampshire
Terence Bellville

The First National Bank
Fair Haven, Vermont
Cecil Forster

Fountain Elms
Utica, New York
Mr. & Mrs. Joseph F. Beard

Buckman Tavern
Lexington, Massachusetts
Mr. & Mrs. Abner Hunt

"Motif #1"
Rockport, Massachusetts
Mr. & Mrs. David Fluke

The Old State House
Boston, Massachusetts
Jennie Hinkle

West Canton Street
Boston, Massachusetts
Richard Clark

The White Horse Tavern
Newport, Rhode Island
Edward J. Brown

Sheldon Street View
Providence, Rhode Island
Mimi McKenzie

Mark Twain's House
Hartford, Connecticut
Ed Zerwekh

Cast-Iron Building in Soho
New York City, New York
Katherine Hellman

The Schnyder House
Quogue, Long Island, New York
Ann Schnyder

Houses on Road 62B
Eureka Springs, Arkansas
Fenn Hathaway

Theatre Center
Oklahoma City, Oklahoma
Michael D. Main

The Stone House
Fayetteville, Arkansas
Terry J. Horton

Rock of Salvation Church
Rahway, New Jersey
Donald Mitchell, O.D.

Main Street House
New Hope, Pennsylvania
Wayne Fabert

Broad Street View
Newark, New Jersey
Mr. & Mrs. Gerard Yablonicky

City Hall
Philadelphia, Pennsylvania
Mr. & Mrs. Rick Ybarra

Spruce Street Houses
Philadelphia, Pennsylvania
Mr. & Mrs. Bobby Schwartz

Hillen Street View
Baltimore, Maryland
Robert & Carol Emerick

The Capitol
Washington, D.C.
Mr. & Mrs. Richard Dart

Charles Herrington's House
Washington, D.C.
Charles Herrington

1307 Rhode Island Avenue N.W.
Washington, D.C.
John Weaver

Don Canty's House
Washington, D.C.
Don Canty

1426 Q Street N.W.
Washington, D.C.
Louis Cipro

Log Cabin
Pickle Fork Holler, Kentucky
Rev. Gene Fisher

Company Store #5
Upper Van Lear, Kentucky
Rev. Gene Fisher

Charles' View of the Murat
Indianapolis, Indiana
Mr. & Mrs. Rick Ybarra

Tim Conley's House
St. Louis, Missouri
Dale T. Craig

2031 Park Avenue
St. Louis, Missouri
Ronald L. Wicks

The Liberty Memorial
Kansas City, Missouri
Kenneth McNames

Kemper Arena
Kansas City, Missouri
Kenneth McNames

House with Gargoyles
Atchison, Kansas
Ed Zerwekh

The Dodge House
Council Bluffs, Iowa
Robert & Carol Emerick

The State Capitol
Des Moines, Iowa
James Shelton, D.D.S.

Tower Grove (The Morton House)
Cedar Rapids, Iowa
Rebecca A. Lloyd

110 E. Mission Street
Strawberry Point, Iowa
Mr. & Mrs. David Pascoe

F. Scott Fitzgerald Row House
St. Paul, Minnesota
Georgie Stillman

Fort Abercrombie
Ft. Abercrombie, North Dakota
Dr. & Mrs. George Bullock

The Corn Palace
Mitchell, South Dakota
Kay Riordan

The Buell Building
Rapid City, South Dakota
Donovan Rypkema

Cucamonga Community Methodist Church
Rancho Cucamonga, California
Mr. & Mrs. Don J. Schmidt

Colorado Street View
Telluride, Colorado
Mr. & Mrs. Rick Ybarra

Davy's View into Telluride
Telluride, Colorado
Faith Brigel

The Red Onion
Aspen, Colorado
Timothy Robert Schropp

Molly Brown's House
Denver, Colorado
Coleman & Kelber, Attys.

The Carissa Mine
near Atlantic City, Wyoming
Coleman & Kelber, Attys.

The Curtiss Music Hall
Butte, Montana
Michael Wayne Sullivan

The Russian Orthodox Cathedral
Sitka, Alaska
Nancy Carlson

Dvorak's Summer House
Bily Clock House
Spillville, Iowa
Patricia Clark

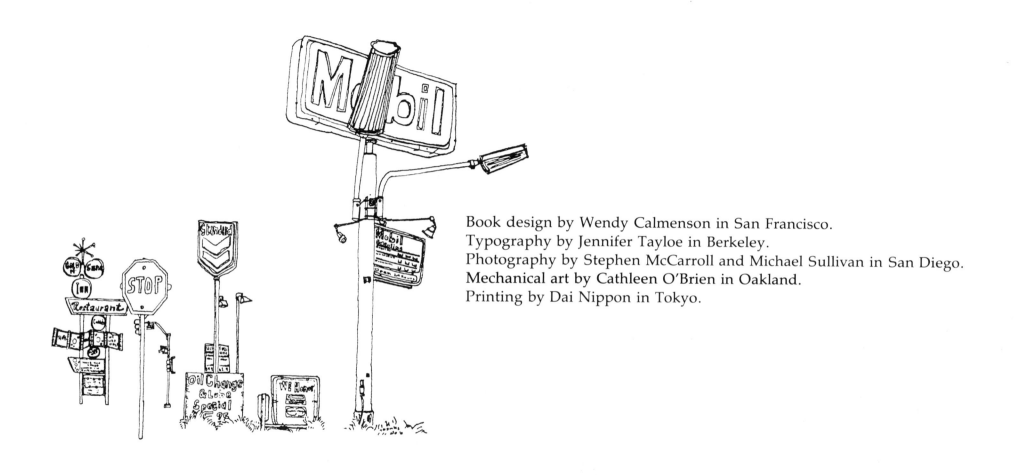

Book design by Wendy Calmenson in San Francisco.
Typography by Jennifer Tayloe in Berkeley.
Photography by Stephen McCarroll and Michael Sullivan in San Diego.
Mechanical art by Cathleen O'Brien in Oakland.
Printing by Dai Nippon in Tokyo.